THE NEW WORD

THE NEW WORD

BY

CHARLES H. GRANDGENT

Essay Index Reprint Series

BOOKS FOR LIBRARIES PRESS
FREEPORT, NEW YORK

First Published 1929
Reprinted 1970

STANDARD BOOK NUMBER:
8369-1707-3

LIBRARY OF CONGRESS CATALOG CARD NUMBER:
75-121471

PRINTED IN THE UNITED STATES OF AMERICA

PREFACE

A NOTE of caution. That the "New Word" in question is disclosed in the title of the opening essay is a natural guess, an easy and time-saving conjecture. But is it therefore true? Haply the real significance of the phrase shall be revealed only to the patient reader who shall push his research to the very end.

At any rate, all the papers in this little volume are new to the printer.

C. H. GRANDGENT

CAMBRIDGE, May, 1929

CONTENTS

THE NEW WORD

GRANDIFUL

"Isn't that lovely?" said Grandma to a three-year-old. "Yes," assented the minute granddaughter, "it's grandiful." Why not? The word is as good a hybrid as a thousand that have butted their way into the dictionary, and it gives full value, combining, as it does, the concepts of beauty and of grandeur. I think it is worth keeping.

So are some of the definitions invented by the same embryonic lexicographer. "A man and a boy was there," she was declaring; "not two men, just a man and a boy." Not quite convinced, her aunt inquired, "What is the difference between a man and a boy?" "Men spank boys," was the prompt and positive answer. How useless it is to deny that our whole *Weltanschauung* is based on social distinctions! Are all men born free and equal? Possibly; but they remain in that grandiful state of equality only as long as they are unspankable. Once the age of spankability sets in, society splits into two strata, the spankers and the spankees, and remains thus cleft until death levels all.

"He's dead," once asserted our Johnsonian midget. "What do you mean by dead?" asked her catechizing aunt. This time a moment's reflection was needed; and here is the outcome: "Smells awful bad."

Yes, death is an ill-smelling thing. That is perhaps its one constant feature. It may be noble, miserable, tragic, common, cruel, welcome; but it is always malodorous, as Hamlet discovered. And children are appalling literalists. I remember a period of my life when the line "Give, freely give, and Heaven will bless your store" always aroused in me the question whether Heaven's blessing descended only on store-keepers. Did other businesses get no reward for charity? Literal the infantile mind is, and specific. The aforementioned interpreter of death is still (she is now four) in the habit of amending a well-known strophe into this:

> I love little pussy,
> Her coat is so warm;
> And if I don't pull her tail,
> She'll do me no harm.

"Hurt her" is weakly vague. "Pull her tail" relates the hypothetical case to one's own experience.

That is the charm of realistic fiction, in print or on the stage. It is Mr. Vincent Crummles's "real pump with real water" that appeals to the infantile mind. Doubtless it has always been so. We do not know— except from a once popular song—what were the "tales that Adam told to Eve." But we can conjecture with some likelihood the reading-matter that was fed to their offspring. There must have been a good boy and a bad boy whose fortunes were appropriately contrasted. Furthermore, it is evident that Abel was led to pattern himself on Sandford, while Cain chose Merton as his model.

Were you brought up on *Sandford and Merton;* and, if so, which did you want to imitate? I had not only Thomas Day's masterpiece, but also John Bunyan's. As far as I can remember, the earliest real book I ever read was a tiny volume, enlivened with woodcuts, called *The Child's Pilgrim's Progress.* So thrilled was I that for years I begged my father to let me have the work unabridged. Vainly he warned me that it would be too much for my appetite; I persisted. When I was six or seven, then, he brought me home a thick volume bound in green. The paper was rather thin, and the print was rather small. There were no pictures. Some conversations there were, to be sure, but they were prevailingly of a too formal character to give much relief. To my credit be it recorded that I put it through, from cover to cover, without skipping. I had asked for it and therefore felt I must eat it.

Almost as filling was a viand accepted shortly afterwards, not against my father's advice but on his recommendation: *The Seven Champions of Christendom,* which, if I am not mistaken, had delighted even Bunyan in his unregenerate youth. The Seven Champions themselves were one hundred percenters;

but the adventures of their sons, nephews, and grandsons, tediously told by a subsequent narrator, put the reader's fortitude to a hard test. Second Parts are always a dubious venture. Have you ever read through the Second Part of *Don Quixote*, or of *Robinson Crusoe*? I have; but I did it at an age which balks at nothing. And when the sequel is written by somebody else, the result is not a venture, but a sure calamity. What a maddening disappointment it was when Fritz—Fritz, my hero, the type of manly independence—went and fell in love with the girl from the strange ship! Not until I learned, in mature life, that the latter part of *The Swiss Family Robinson* is not by the hand of the original author did I become in a measure reconciled to Fritz's weak conventionality. Probably, after all, it wasn't true. Still, there was that damning picture of the gyurl on her knees before Mrs. Swiss Family Robinson (I think Fritz is with her) crying, "O mother, mother, pray forgive me!" No, I will not believe it. That part of the story is spurious.

As soon as I saw that picture, I had a foreboding of shattered idols. Of course I always began a book—if it was illustrated—by looking at all the illustrations. Presumably all children do. Then I began reading around the most interesting ones. After that, my perusal would spread out and out from each of these foci, like a grease spot, until in places the circumferences touched. That was the time to go back to the beginning and take the whole in due form. My volume of *The Swiss Family Robinson* was a very beautiful one, clear in type and rich in pictorial adornment. But there was one horribly vexatious thing about it. The illustrations were taken from two previous editions, whose editors had harbored diametrically opposed conceptions of some of the characters. In the colored plates taken (I believe) from a German source, Mr. Swiss Family Robinson was a fine, handsome man with a full beard; whereas the black-and-white cuts, of French extraction, portrayed him consistently as a rather squatty, commonplace person with side whiskers. Not all my very considerable ingenuity could devise means of unifying this dual personality; nor could penciled mustache and chin-hair on the offending cuts reconcile the two hostile types. Mr. S. F. R. continued to live a double life, an embodiment of the eternal conflict between the Romantic and the Realistic.

Romanticism and Realism do not succeed each other, as the text-books say; they exist side by side. Sometimes one is on the surface, sometimes the other, but they are both there all the time. Nowadays an author writes prose and tries to make the public believe it is verse; when I was a boy, the poet wrote poetry and his interpreter would turn it into prose. The supreme triumph of an old-time elocutionist was to recite a long, rimed poem in such fashion that not a hearer should suspect it was aught else than prose; whereas our present-day poet will read you a still longer bit of his own prose with a gentle metronomic swaying of his body and a singsong intonation that shall give something of the illusion of verse. In our era, be it noted, the poet has to be his own elocutionist; *troubadour* and *jongleur* are one. It must be so; for whatever rhythm the author has, he does not put into his lines, but keeps to himself. Nobody else, then, can phrase him aright.

The elocutionist, though not extinct, is obsolescent. I am glad that he (and especially she) is obsolescent, but I am glad also that the tribe has not entirely disappeared. The best instruction in English I ever received was given me by an itinerant elocution teacher, who at stated intervals visited the grammar school where I was a pupil; I am glad to record his name—Moses True Brown. His method was closer to the French *analyse de textes* than anything else I have seen in this country. By a simple system of pencil marks he taught us to indicate in our books the varied intonations; but the why and wherefore of the intonations was the important thing. Sentence by sentence, line by line, he would dissect a poem, showing the connection of member with member, the relation of phrase to phrase. Why did the poet use this expression rather than that? Why did he put this word at the beginning and not at the end? Was it a matter of logical stress or of metrics? Such were the fascinating questions he raised. Perhaps he was not infallible in his answers; all the same, the questions were asked, and the habit of questioning was implanted.

In my freshman year in college I came under the guidance of another elocutionist. It was not George Riddle; you remember Riddle, who, after so brilliant a success as an amateur, met with defeat on the professional stage. I always attributed his ill luck to the play. Who wrote *The Earl*, I have forgotten; and what it was like, I never rightly knew. But it was an unalluring title. It sounds like howling, and I cannot picture the interpreter of Œdipus as a good howler. Sothern, to be sure, was not at his best in ululation, yet he made a success of *The Prisoner of Zenda*, which had more howls in it than Hagenbeck's menagerie. Well, Riddle was too good a sport to put the blame on the piece; he simply announced that he "had been trampled upon by the proverbially big feet of Boston."

No, this was a gentleman named Ticknor, who taught us many useful things. But he cherished one superstition universal in his craft at that time, and not yet forgotten; to wit, that *er* and *ur* should be pronounced differently—for instance, in *serf* and *surf*. Each profession, it would seem, has its pet trick of pronunciation. None but the old-fashioned actor puts two *v*'s into *never*; the clergyman alone makes *great* sound like a much drawled *grat*; only sailor-folk and their kin say *no-thard*; the race of mechanics has a monopoly of *taycle* for *tackle*; the elocutionist is the exclusive proprietor of the aforesaid nice distinction, which cannot be conveyed in print. His notion (I may add parenthetically) comes from a misunderstanding of some 18th-century orthoëpists; it is too intricate a business to be allowed admission here. Well, Mr. Ticknor one day wrote on the board the two words, *pearl* and *purl*, and asked every member of the class how he pronounced them. Most of the fellows, with some hesitancy, sounded them alike, suspecting a trick, but seeing no escape. Others, sure of a "ketch," said *perl* and *poorl*. One member, who afterwards won distinction as a financier and statesman, tortured the second word into *poo-erl*, thus precociously displaying that genius for compromise which marks the politician.

I suppose the elocutionary shibboleth might have extended itself, had it appealed to some very prominent speaker—prominent enough to set a style; it might then have become epidemic, like the British version of *girl*, or the American *att all*. Fashion enslaves the world. "We all like sheep," as the good song says. A decade or two ago, we all ran to have our appendix out if our tooth ached; now a pain in the belly calls for the extraction of a tooth. We move in a body, as if worked by one set of springs. Traffic regulations, which compel us all to do the same thing at the same moment, are merely an outward manifestation of our innate gregariousness. Advertising has not only destroyed the last vestiges of privacy but

has also robbed us of free will. Dimly conscious of
having become a race of robots, we cannot bear to
think that man has ever been a genuinely self-
regulating machine. There has arisen a school of
biography whose special mission it is to soothe our
vanity by showing us that the conspicuous men of the
past were really as commonplace as you and I. Thus
we have a de-Lincolnized Lincoln, a George Washington with the Washington cut out and nothing
left but George, a vulgarized Jesus Christ. By the
way, did you notice, last winter, that the Christmas
cards, so beautiful, so ingenious, and so varied in
their decoration, nearly all agreed in one feature—
the omission of any reference to the event which
Christmas is supposed to commemorate?

The more flivverlike we become, the less tolerant
are we of any other make. We come to love the banal,
we cultivate a preference for the second-rate, we
choose the substitute. Recently I attended, with
four or five hundred other guests, a banquet given
in honor of a foreign Ambassador. There were two
toastmasters, a general and a judge, the decision
having been reached, apparently, that no one living
man was adequate to such an emprise. His Excellency
was present; and so was the genial Mayor, who, as
far as I could make out, having succeeded in dodging
the delegation at noon, thought it only fair to sacrifice himself in the evening. The other speakers were
all substitutes. Every introduction began with a note

of regret. "I am very sorry to announce that the
Governor has been unexpectedly called from town,
but in his stead he has sent the always popular
Secretary, whom I take pleasure in presenting."
"General B. fully intended to be with us, but a sore
throat has compelled him to avail himself of the
competent services of General J." "The President of
the Chamber of Commerce, prevented at the last
moment from joining us, has induced the Vice-Presi-
dent, whom you all know so well, to take his place."
"A press of business has made it impossible for the
Chief Justice of the Superior Court to accept our
invitation. He has, however, sent us as his representative the Associate Justice, whom you will be glad to
hear." And so we were; for he made a good speech.
But the whole affair suggested a box of Assorted
Seconds. I speak without personal feeling, for, although I had a seat at the speakers' table, I was
neither a first nor a second (there were no thirds). I
recall the scene only as a symbolic picture of the
Age of Substitutes.

After-dinner oratory is exposed, no doubt, to
further standardization, when it shall all be supplied,
like political speeches, from a few radio stations.
That expectation will bring refreshment to many a
tired soul. I suppose that, within certain limits, the
difficulty of public performance is in inverse ratio to
the audience. It is easiest, of course, on the stage,
where the performer is assured of undivided atten-

tion: enshrined in a spot-light, he is the only possible focus; the auditors, relaxed and isolated, are prevented by darkness from counting the flies on the wall. At a banquet the job is harder; there are too many things to look at, and the parties of the second part are too conscious of themselves and of one another. Most difficult is the lot of the impromptu drawing-room entertainer, for his hearers are likely to be thinking more of themselves and their neighbors than of him, conceiving perhaps some clever thing to say when they shall have a chance, if only the everlasting talker will stop before they forget it. "I should be very glad to answer any questions," declared a lecturer at the close of a rather prolonged discourse. "Would anyone like to ask a question?" "Yes," said a sleepy-looking man in the front row. "What time is it?"

The offer to answer inquiries is a convenient way to close an address, if you can think of no more dramatic *dénouement*. But it opens fearful possibilities. Perhaps it is better to use the copperplate phrase, "I thank you." For although the user of this formula generally has grounds for gratitude (having escaped without shooting), his words are very seldom expression of that sentiment. They mean simply: "Finis. Explicit. The End. You have no further cause for apprehension. There isn't any more; that's all." Yet there is nothing else so reassuring as the good old curtain. And in spite of radio, victrola, and movies, there is no show like the regular old stage show, a real play with real people. To my mind, the modern substitutes can no more replace it than vaudeville can take the place of sawdust and canvas.

Soon after the Civil War (I hate to say how soon after) I saw a piece called *The Union Spy*. It was in Lewiston, Maine; and it made a firm impression because it was one of my earliest theatrical experiences. Like one of Shakespere's chronicle plays, it embraced the whole history of the epoch. It is evident, then, that the action had to be rapid, and that little time could be wasted on superfluous dialogue. There was just room for a funny man and a very condensed hero. I remember Fort Sumter with great distinctness, and Andersonville Prison; but the piece was chiefly made up of battle scenes. They had to be quick battles, else some of the encounters of the Civil War would have had to be omitted. Moreover, they were all constructed on the same pattern. Let me describe it. Sixteen supernumeraries did the fighting; eight trimly dressed men in blue on one side, eight rather seedy chaps in gray, with flapping sombreros, on the other. Six shots would be fired, off stage, on the left. Presently the gray squad would trot across the stage from left to right, pursued at an even pace by the blues. Six shots would then be heard in the right wings; whereupon the blues would trot across first, followed by the grays. Thunder on the left, consisting of six

shots more. Reverse again. And so it went on, with
three alternations for the lesser engagements, seven
for the great battles.

I have introduced this stirring theme, not for the
mere excitement of it, but because these to-and-fro
collective trots so aptly represent the flux of fashion,
a subject to which I am endeavoring to return. In
particular, they are a pat figure of the alternating
pursuit of woman by man and man by woman. All
of us who are old enough to count in this world can
recall a time when it was the style for the female to
retreat and for the male to chase. Then, with no
thunder on left save the production of Shaw's *Man
and Superman*, the tide turned. A good view of present
conditions can be had at our American State Uni-
versities, which are all of the bi-sexual type. In these
seats of learning (perhaps "standing room only"
would be a better name), Eve at the very beginning
drove Adam out of all the "culture" courses. In
terror Adam fled into economics and government,
but Eve followed him there; he retreated into chemistry, into physics, into engineering, and lo! Eve
was there.

Nor did the hunt confine itself to the sacred groves
of Academe. Where is now the safe seclusion of the
smoking car? Where the mystery of the barber's
shop? What can man do henceforth, unless he let
his hair and beard grow long, and frequent only
those places where smoking is forbidden? The results

of the new invasion are by no means all seen as yet—
the literary results, for instance. Who ever could have
prophesied the disappearance of the *Police Gazette*
from the tonsorial parlor, the familiar old *Police
Gazette*, condemned by pudibund capillary artists as
unsafe for feminine perusal? O useless precaution!

Did you ever listen to a barbers' choir? In Cambridge, at the corner of Garden Street and Phillips
Place, we have a new hotel; and about half of its
ground floor is occupied by a very large and attractive
tonsorial establishment. As I was walking hurriedly
by, one morning early, I seemed to hear all the
barbers warbling together, with exceeding sweetness.
"Is it a substitute for conversation?" I asked myself.
"Perhaps the proprietor compels them to sing, just
as the boy has to whistle while he is bringing in the
sweets." But I had no time to investigate. Another
morning I heard the same sweet harmony; all the
barbers singing together like the morning stars. I
pictured each artist standing open-mouthed behind
his respective chair, pouring forth his soul in melody,
while his customer either listened in silent and foamy
admiration or parted his lathered lips to join in the
chorus. Again, keen as my curiosity was, I had no
opportunity to peer in. The third time, however, I
could endure it no longer; I paused to investigate.
Amazement! The tonsorial palace was absolutely
empty. But still the glad chorus issued forth. Could
the barbers be chirping in concealment, like tree-

toads or like young frogs in the spring? One seldom
sees a katydid, I thought. Can there be a hidden
relationship between katydids and barbers? The
truth (for truth will out) was less poetic, as I presently discovered. On the opposite corner is a school
for boys; and when the pupils sing their matins, the
sound is echoed across the narrow street from the
high hotel building, as if it came from within. The
barbers, then, were singing *in absentia*, with voices not
their own.

How much of what we say is our own, and how
much is echo? We listen every day to "political
arguments," which consist in the repetition, by
each participant, of the leading articles (or, more
likely, the headlines) in his particular newspaper. Is
anyone ever converted by this process? Man is
defined as the "rational animal," and rightly. But
he uses his reason, not to form his opinions, but to
defend them, to himself and others, after they are
formed. Their basis is not logical deduction but
emotion and prejudice. Argument cannot shake him,
nothing but an appeal to passion or prejudice will
make him change. And his arguments will be good,
and his opponent's will be good; because both are
"rational animals."

We can always find good reasons for swimming with
the tide; and the tide changes twice a day. So do our
standards rise and fall. Half a century ago, when
I first visited Bethlehem, New Hampshire, a more

experienced friend, showing me the sights, pointed
out the Sinclair Hotel, then at the apex of grandeur,
and declared in a tone of awe: "People in that house
pay seventeen dollars a week!" Some years later, that
same friend and I, in a hotel at the seashore, were
filled with equal awe, and even greater admiration,
in the contemplation of a certain Mr. Cunningham,
a favorite guest. He was a spry, vivacious, cheery
gentleman, who could sail a boat, and row, and walk,
and drive a horse, with the best. And he was fifty-
five years old! (This incident will afford amusement
in proportion to the reader's age.) Who shall stand-
ardize the standards? Mr. Hinchman, in his *Pedes-
trian Papers*, tells of a man entering an eating-house
which bore this sign: "Pies and coffee like mother
used to make." "Are your pies and coffee really like
mother used to make?" he inquired dubiously.
"Exactly!" assures the proprietor. "Then I guess I'll
have toast and tea."

Time is not the only alterer of styles and standards:
place alters them, too. The type of the heavy drinker
is a fish, with us; in France, it is a duck. I once was
trying to turn into English verse a lovely passage
from Dante. On the last stairway of the Purgatorial
mountain, at eve, the poet is about to fall asleep,
between his two guides, whom he likens to herdsmen
watching over their flocks. Himself, he pictures as
the safely guarded animal—a *capra*, or goat. Now is
it possible to say, in American English, "I was the

goat," without disturbing the poetic atmosphere? At any rate, I followed Abraham's example, and substituted a sheep. Yet in Italy, as in France, the goat, a symbol of agility, has no suggestion of the grotesque. In England, whatever he may be now, he was not ludicrous in the time of Laurence Sterne; Maria's goat adds a romantic touch. But, in our country the creature still retains the odor of defunct Shantytown. So it goes. What is comic in one land, in another may be grandiful.

MOSTLY ABOUT EATING

"WHEN this is done," quotes *Punch* from a cook-book, "sit on a very hot stove, and stir frequently." "Who wouldn't?" Mr. Punch inquires. At any rate, Mr. Welland Strong did—the Dying Man, in *A Trip to Chinatown*. Why doesn't somebody revive those old "farce comedies" of Hoyt's? Sitting on a hot stove may not be the acme of humor, but it is funnier than most of the "revue" stuff. And there was a good deal more than that in Hoyt, or Howells would never have been so fond of him. What a character was Jonah, in *A Brass Monkey*, as George Marion played him! And when shall we hear the like of the Razzle Dazzle trio again?

As far as heat goes, I suppose electric stoves and coal stoves and gas stoves offer about the same seating facilities; but gas stoves seem to have the heaviest appetites. How the old meter does spin! Once I made up my mind the recording apparatus must be out of order; I ought to do something about it. Under this conviction I called at the gas office and testified to my belief. "Wait a moment, please," said the attendant, politely, "until I call Mr. Salisbury." Presently Mr. Salisbury appeared, a tall, portly, majestic gentleman, with a full beard, immaculate attire, a low, soft voice, and a manner caressingly courteous. He listened to my complaint with an indulgent smile. When I had quite finished, "Kindly follow me," he said, "into the adjoining room." There, on the wall, was a demonstration meter, which could be taken all to pieces and put together again. Which Mr. Salisbury proceeded to do, with a minute explanation that seemed to be clarity itself. Round and round my poor head swam, as one mystery followed another. Even if I had understood the outlandish words, I am sure I never could have guessed what they were doing. And still the honied stream flowed on, submerging me deeper and deeper. "Now you see," he concluded, "how utterly impossible is any inaccuracy in that mechanism." "Yes, sir," said I, meekly picking up my hat. I had my revenge, though, a few months later, when, for a wonder, the meter developed a halting disposition, and week after week left its hands uplifted in the same attitude of prayer. Remembering Mr. Salisbury's statement, I decided that nothing was to be done. But the company, when it found out, thought differently. I think the physicists must be mistaken when they say that no speed can be greater than the velocity of light. They ought to have seen the quickness with which that good old sympathetic meter was cast out by a metrical whipper-snapper quite devoid of human feeling.

Here is the human touch, in a sign on an all-night
restaurant: "Try our coffee. We never sleep." As
far as my experience goes, though, tea is just as
persistent as coffee in its warning of "sleep no more!"
The tea-drinker gets all the wages of sin without any
of the fun. Of course, some people are simply driven
to sinfulness. I mean the English, whose coffee is so
peculiar that they have to drink tea for breakfast.
How bad English coffee is, I never fully grasped
(although I had occasionally sampled it) until I
read in one of Max Beerbohm's essays a paean of
delight that he is starting for Paris, where he can get
a good cup of coffee. If French coffee can taste good
to anyone (and an epicure at that), consider what
he must have at home! Vienna used to drink real
coffee in the days before the war, and Constantinople
still does; elsewhere they have some nauseous bean
whose nastiness the French wisely drown in chicory.

Breakfast is a ticklish meal; your appetite depends
so much on your intake the evening before. For me,
as a steady diet, I find coffee, bread, and fruit a good
program. But I like almost anything, except breakfast foods. About once or twice a twelvemonth, indeed,
I can join my countrymen in chops and griddle
cakes. That was my mood, one morning, years ago,
on a Maine steamer. I was hungry; and I ordered
steak, French fried potatoes, and rolls. My steak—a
huge one—had just come in, when President and
Mrs. Eliot entered and took seats directly opposite

me. Their order, for the two, was one shredded
wheat. What was a man to do? Should I sit there
and stuff myself with meat and vegetable while
they were ascetically nibbling at their shredded
wheat? Should I offer them a portion of my amply
sufficient steak, thus disparaging by implication
their own provision? Should I affect an indifference
I was far from feeling, leave my steak untouched, and
simply toy with a bit of potato? What would you
have done?

A hungry man is a great container; but he is a
pill-box compared to a toad or a robin. In the
experimental days of boyhood I spent a whole afternoon trying to fill up a toad. I was fond of these
creatures. I liked their gentle disposition and their
beautiful eyes; and I never would accept the doctrine
that they give you warts. Warts enough they have, in
all conscience; but they never part with any of them.
Now, a toad—like a lizard or a spider—cares only for
live food. You must put before him some moving
thing; and as soon as he sees it stir, out shoots his
long, sticky tongue, and in goes the worm. Quite
startling is the velocity with which the transfer is
made. Equally amazing is the immediate readiness
for another operation. There the creature sits,
tranquil and immobile as a Buddha, and with the
Buddha's never changing smile. Nor does the Buddha-
like abdominal rotundity seem to increase as the
tireless tongue darts to and fro. Amusing at first, my

task becomes unending as the labor of Sisyphus. I denude our garden of caterpillars and all else that creeps. I deplete the gardens of the neighbors. Is the monster satisfied? Silent and serene he squats, and gives no sign.

A robin is just as receptive. A young one, apparently an orphan, too immature to fly from cats, was picked up in our yard, and we tried to keep it alive. So we did, for about a week, but the whole family, working in relays, was kept busy all day digging worms. Fortunately no night shifts were needed, or we should have struck. Earthworms poured into that hungry beak like water into Baron Munchausen's truncated horse. At last the poor little creature died, not of hypertrophy, but of a sort of creeping paralysis. We mourned its demise; but we sat down to do so.

A chameleon lizard, which some one sent us from the South, proved to be much less exigent quantatively but deplorably fastidious. We kept him through an autumn and a winter. A pretty little beast he was, innocent and enterprising. He wore his heart, so to speak, on his sleeve; for he changed hue according to his moods, from bright green in happiness or excitement, to dark brown in moments of chilly gloom, with an intermediate stage of trout-like speckles. Although he had a beautiful home, a great glass-lidded box, filled with verdure, he would occasionally give us the slip, and, hiding on the inner edge of some table-cloth or other hanging, would make himself invisible by assuming its color; sometimes he eluded detection for days. Such escapades, though we forgave them, were hard to bear. Hardest, however, was his absolute scorn of immobile refection. The choicest insects never interested him, unless they crawled or flew. I became incredibly expert at catching things on the wing—even mosquitos—without damaging them. Once I secured a wasp, which he, after a thrilling contest, conquered and absorbed. As the weather grew colder, and wild life scarce, I discovered cheap restaurants where flies lingered later than elsewhere. These haunts (much to the damage of my digestion) I frequented, armed with a little paper cage in which I imprisoned my prey. But there came a season when even the untidiest joints were flyless. The only resource then was the cultivation of meal-worms. You buy some meal, you let it grow moist and mouldy; and after a while certain white, slow-creeping, unappetizing worms appear. These the lizard did not really like (and I could not rightly blame him), but from time to time he would reluctantly gather one in—just enough to save him from starvation. During those months he wore his darkest brown. Tragic was his end. As spring approached, his adventurous temper awoke again, and he fell a victim to the cat.

Man needs but little for breakfast, and he eats that little dead. Yet he is seldom capable of providing it unaided. When a man is deserted by his whole family in June, and has to live by his wits, he finds them strangely insufficient. For luncheon and dinner he can go to a restaurant or a club, but he hates to go out for his initial meal. On the other hand, he is inexpert at cooking and impatient of dish-washing. In stories of adventure, people who are lost in the woods live on "roots and berries." I have always wondered what kind of roots; elm, maple, and birch I know to be inadequate. I did live, though, for a fortnight on bananas and olives, which I had seen recommended in some book of travel. A relative, who happened to call at the house, found me in the last stages of extenuation. And I did not care for olives or bananas for a long time thereafter. Another year, I hit upon a new labor-saving diet: cherries and beer. The beer I had in my cellar, and the cherries I picked as needed, from a tree behind the house. It was my own tree; but I had to fight with the robins for every cherry. How I repented of ever having tried to save the life of one of those harpies! The beverage, like Mrs. Gummage's, was both mild and regular, being safe (in those ante-Volstead days) from competitive enterprise.

When Maine's sobriety was in her own keeping, she used to allow the sale of a supposedly non-intoxicating "three per cent. beer." This was offered, to cite one example, in a shed on a wharf in that strictly maritime and railroadless town, Boothbay Harbor;

and thither, occasionally, my mate and I used to betake ourselves when we had made that port on a thirsty day. Early one season, when we had repaired to this haven, and had comfortably installed ourselves, particularly in the mood for rest and cheerfulness, we observed that the picturesque, solemn old keeper, whom we had indissolubly associated with the place, was absent; and we inquired of the new functionary what had become of him. "Gone, sir," the successor answered dismally. "Gone for long?" we asked. "Forever," was the reply. After a portentous pause, he continued: "We come in one mornin', just like it was today, and we found him a-layin' stark and stiff on the ground, starin' up at the ceilin'. Dead as a door-nail. He laid right acrost the floor. I kin almost see him now. His head was just about where you're a-settin', sir, with his eyes fixed and starin' straight upwards." I gave my chair an uneasy hitch. "Yes, sir, that's the very spot. When I look at it, I kin see his face still." If we had stayed longer, we should have been seeing it ourselves.

A regular tragedian's face, that man had. I wonder whether character shapes faces, or faces fashion character. I seem to have read somewhere—perhaps in William James—that our physical reactions precede our mental ones. We have learned from Coué the value of persistent optimism of phrase and look. If expression determines emotion, how happy chorus girls must be! Two things certainly do go together:

pretty teeth and a sense of humor. If you want an appreciative auditor for a funny story, tell it to a lady whose dentition is faultless. Perhaps even our tragic three per center was capable of assuming at times a jovial air and with it a jocular temper. We are too apt to think that people are all of a piece. If a man is wrong (that is, differs from us) in one respect, he must be perverse in everything. I can remember a time when I believed that all democrats were homeopaths; the bottom of the universe seemed to have dropped out when I discovered an allopathic democrat. We are in the habit of blaming the sunspots for our bad weather, never once conceiving that there may be good sunspots which cause our good weather. All sunspots are to us homoeopathic and democratic.

What a shock it is when the mystery of "Fly away Jack" and "Fly away Jill" is first uncovered, and we learn that different fingers play the parts! What a triumph when it dawns on us that in the game of tit-tat-too you cannot be beaten if you have the first turn! Then there is that favorite though unsavory game in which one child suddenly remarks: "I saw a dead horse in the road. I one it." His companion responds: "I two it." The first continues: "I three it." And so on, until the unfortunate second has to say: "I eight it." I can still feel my thrill of delight when I found out (somewhat in advance of my playmates) that the propounder of the numerical sequence always wins.

Memory is a capricious thing. Why is it that we recall the trifling incidents of childhood so much more clearly than the momentous events of later years? Partly, of course, it is because the records of infancy are written on a clean slate. But there is another reason: as we grow older, we become more and more convinced that most things are not worth remembering, and consequently we cease to store them. The old oaken bucket remains, while subsequent silver cups melt away.

Ever memorable are those shows for children which used to be offered gratuitously by the city on the Fourth of July. There was the comic vocalist who sang *The Monks of Old* and *Who Stole the Donkey?* There was the miracle-making prestidigitator, with his endless ribbon and his hat-dwelling rabbits; not to speak of the ventriloquist. There was the learned pig, spelling out with cards the answers to questions. There was a two-headed colored girl, who sang duets. And (joy of joys!) there was one year the children's idol, Paul Du Chaillu, the African explorer.

Childhood had its sorrows too, its dreary failures, almost too heart-rending to tell. Here is one of them, though. My cousins were about to make a visit, and I was bent on producing in our attic a spectacular fairy play of my own devising. When children want a thing, they want it with all their hearts and all their minds. For this performance I needed a distant light in a dark forest; I believe it was to emanate

from a witch's cottage, but all that was required was
a bright spot in the midst of blackness. Now, my
mother would not allow me to play with lamps,
candles, or matches. I could obtain a considerable
degree of obscurity by closing the blinds; but that
speck of light—whence could it be drawn? At last
the idea came to me (a flash of inspiration from
above) that light could be conducted from out-of-
doors through a long paper tube and released at the
point required. A chink in a shutter served as an
inlet. For the tube I needed white paper, smooth and
stiff enough to take and retain cylindrical shape, and
sufficiently thick to keep the light from escaping.
This was not easy to obtain; but I finally got something that nearly met the requirements, though it
scarcely sufficed in quantity and had to be supple-
mented by inferior material. I decided that the
conduit must be straight, for light could not be
trusted (in the days before Einstein) to turn around a
corner. Even so, the construction of that tube was no
easy problem. Should it be held together by string, or
pins, or paste? Before the end, I tried all these ex-
pedients, but none with complete success. You see,
the channel must be made tight, so that the lumi-
nousness should not leak out on the way; yet the
passage must not be obstructed by crushing. All one
afternoon I labored feverishly; all the next morning,
at a still higher temperature; all the following afternoon, with growing desperation. When I had finished,

the day was too far spent for a test. You can well conceive that sleep shunned my pillow that night. Early in the morning I was afoot to make the great trial. Luckily the day was sunny; but alas! it brought no sunshine to me. The outcome was worse than my worst foreboding. Brightness in abundance streamed in through the cracks in the shutters, while from the end of my conductor emerged no illumination whatever. Nothing but blackness in the tube, nothing but blackness in my heart. Too broken to cry, I closed the door of my attic playroom. It was many a month before I had courage to open it again.

Not all failures are so wrapped in gloom; and few, I fancy, are so unique as my experiment in conducting light. Surely, many a vintner has fallen short of perfection in the concoction of wine. No shame, then, on my cousin Ellery and me for our shortcoming. We had seen pictures of European countryfolk treading out the grapes; and we had watched the process of Yankee cider-making. What more was needed? One requisite, to be sure, was a tub; and a tub we got—not the new wash-tub, which my aunt was unwilling to relinquish, but an old one, deservedly discarded and a bit mouldy from long seclusion in the cellar. This receptacle we filled with wild grapes, easily obtainable from neighboring stone walls, if you managed to keep clear of the poison ivy. Then came the trampling, the most attractive part of the business; and we went at it with might and main.

How the juice did squirt! One detail we had missed,
perhaps because our pictorial models were on too
small a scale; we had not observed that in trans-
Atlantic vineyards the treaders are bare-footed.
Possibly we assumed that European peasants are too
poor to buy shoes. At any rate, we had plunged into
our vat, boots and all. It was a bit disquieting to see
how the blacking came off, and our footgear turned
brown, then yellow, then a sickly white. Still we kept
bravely on. When there seemed to be no occasion for
more stamping, we stepped out, dripping, and poured
forth the copious juice. This we strained into a large
earthen jar, filtering it through a cloth that we had
picked up somewhere. Fermentation was the next stage,
and that must be left to nature. To assure absolute
purity, we put in, I believe, neither yeast nor sugar.
Three or four times a day we would inspect our
future Falernian; but there was never a sign of stir.
Not a bubble to betray inner perturbation. Gradually, however, its surface began to take on the
aspect of a swampy frog-pond. A greenish yellow
scum accumulated on top, and thickened day by
day. Was the liquid really turning into wine under
that impenetrable screen? Neither of us could
screw his courage to the tasting point, although each
vigorously encouraged the other to do so. From that
day to this, indeed, it has remained unsampled. If it
still exists, in the dark corner of the cellar into which
we eventually shoved it, the fluid may have developed

a deliciousness beyond compare. Sometime it may come to light and astonish the world, that vintage of 1876.

Meanwhile we must rest satisfied with cherries and beer. I have said that the tree from which I got my cherries, that June, was my own. Have you ever plucked cherries from a tree that was not your own? If you are addicted to that sin, listen to the following tale, and be cured ere it is too late. At the corner of Amory Street, near the New England·Hospital, was a vacant lot; and across that lot ran diagonally a path so well worn that it seemed like a public way. Now, right beside that well-worn path, one day in my childhood, there stood a well-worn little cherry-tree, stripped of most of its foliage and of all its fruit save one forlorn cherry, which still dangled temptingly from an upper bough, inviting capture. Capture was quickly effected by means of a stone, and the cherry—the ill-gotten cherry—was in my pocket. At this juncture I observed bearing down on me from the rear an elderly man whose expression boded no good. To my childish eye he was a duplicate of the miser in *The Chimes of Normandy*. I quickened my pace; he quickened his. There could be no further doubt of his hostile intention. I broke into a run; so did he, chasing me at full tilt down Amory Street. He never could have caught me, though, had it not been for those three fat brewers, who at an evil moment stepped out of their brewery, and, ranging them-

selves on the side of law and order, formed a solid
block across the road. How I shuddered when I felt
the pursuer's bony fingers clutch my collar! *Come mi
riscossi*—just as Guido da Montefeltro did, gripped by
the fiend! "Vot hess he tun?" inquired one of the
beery interferers, with a stupid grin. "Hookin'
cherries," answered my captor laconically, being
still very short of breath. Vainly did I point out to
him the inaccuracy of his plural, producing from
my pocket as evidence the pitiful *corpus delicti*, and
eagerly offering complete restitution. "Not on your
life," he panted. "You boys hev bothered me to
death, stealin' my cherries. Naow I've caught ye, and
I'm goin' to make an example of ye." "What are you
going to do to me?" I timidly asked. "I'm goin' to
take ye to the Police Station, and hev the law on ye,"
was the savage rejoinder. "What's your name, and
where do ye live?" he demanded. With infantile in-
genuousness I gave a truthful answer. Too late I
repented of my candor. For, terrible as was the
mental image of my pale face peering out between
thick prison bars, still more awful was the thought of
disgrace to my family. I pictured the glaring headlines on the front page of the *Boston Journal*, an-
nouncing that Charles, son of So-and-So, had been
arrested for theft, tried, convicted, sentenced, and
sent to jail. In despair I begged my tyrant to leave
my punishment to the severe hand of my father.
The suggestion met with no response.

At this critical moment there hove in sight two brawny lads of eighteen or thereabouts, unknown to me but evidently belonging to that class which I had always previously, in somewhat terrified disparagement, designated as "toughs." They stepped in front of us, and bade us halt. "What are ye doin' to our little brudder?" asked one of them, not threateningly but sternly. "He's ben a-hookin' my cherries," replied a voice just a bit faltering. "Micky," said the spokesman of the twain, addressing me with an air of reproof, "don't ye know ye hadn't never ought to steal? It's wicked. We'll have to punish ye for that, when we get home." "Did ye call him Micky?" inquired the cherry-owner, with sudden suspicion. "That ain't the name he gin me." "Michael Clarence Mulcahy is his right name. If he says it's anything else, he's a liar. Look here, Micky, have ye been tellin' lies, besides stealin'? Haven't I told ye, many's the time, ye must always tell the troot? We'll have to settle wid ye for that. You leave him to us, mister. We'll see that he gets what's comin' to him, and he won't never trouble ye no more." The captor hesitated. He hated to relinquish his prey; but what was he to do? He was no match for either of these boys, who were closing in on us with a mien that discouraged refusal. Slowly and reluctantly he detached his fingers from my neck, while my two rescuers grasped me tight, one by each arm. Thus they marched me off, until the enemy was out of sight. Then, releasing me, they cried: "Run home now, sonny! And don't let that old divil catch ye again." In an ecstasy of relief, I once more fished from my pocket the forbidden fruit, now in a distinctly dilapidated condition, and offered it as a token of gratitude. Kindly but decidedly they declined the gift, and pursued their way.

I am now soliciting contributions for a monument to The Hoodlum. But already I have misgivings. Monuments seldom convey to the next generation the sentiment that erected them. Can it be that our memorials of the World War will look as absurd to the people of the future as the mementos of our Civil Conflict appear to us? Can anything within our power of conceiving ever reach the depth of bathos achieved by that omnipresent undersized soldier, with long hair and drooping mustache, kepi-hatted and cape-overcoated, leaning lackadaisically on a musket at the top of a column? No, my Hoodlum shall be exposed to no such risk. Let me end this paper as I began it, with a wise dictum of the British Mentor. Commenting on a report that the Round Pond in Kensington Gardens is under consideration as a site for a statue, Mr. Punch prudently asks: "But is the Pond deep enough?"

HABIT

It is not Conscience that makes cowards of us all: it is Habit. Why does John Doe shrink from murder? Because it has never become a part of his daily dozen, and it is not generally done in his set. Why is Richard Roe afraid to stop drinking? Simply because he has forgotten what it is to go to bed sober, and he has a horror of the unknown. Habit it is that makes us good or bad, gentle or coarse, prudish or shameless, civilized or savage. Taine has defined the individual as a bundle of sensations. Let us say rather a bundle of habits, which control the individual's acts and thoughts, like the wires that move a puppet.

Should the question arise, whence come our habits, the answer is obvious: they come from other habits, and especially the habits of other people. Habits propagate by imitation, quite as do the characters in novels and in the drama, who are all the offspring of other imaginary personages. Or, to change the figure, habits may be likened to contagious diseases, to epidemics, which spread with incredible velocity to a whole nation, or (like influenza) to the whole world. How they start, no man can say; who knows the genesis of measles? Nor can any human being prophesy how or when a given habit shall end.

Some people think they can tell you the origin of our present national fashion of lawlessness; they will assure you, with tears in their eyes, that it began with the Eighteenth Amendment. Nonsense! It throve long before that. A more plausible theory would impute it to the Fourth of July. I do not mean the genuine 1776 Declaration, but the successive annual celebrations thereof. Every year the tender youth of our country is encouraged to express its patriotism in terms of crime: in hellish din, menacing the very existence of the sick, the nerves of the industrious, and the temper of all who survive; in the reckless use of dangerous explosives, which frequently blow to pieces not only the users, but innocent bystanders; in wanton theft and destruction of signs, gates, shutters, and everything else that is detachable and combustible. Does the Glorious Fourth stand for anything historical in the mind of the celebrants? Not a bit of it. It is simply a day when everyone may with impunity be a thug. And not only with impunity; with a certain aroma of sanctity. It is a quasi-religious thuggery. (This paragraph was written the day after the Fourth.)

Now, I am not one of those one-theory fanatics who cannot abide anyone else's fanaticisms. I grant you that the National Holiday, while responsible for 99 per cent. of our criminal tendencies, cannot justly be held to account for all. I am willing, indeed, to admit that Prohibition has exercised a fostering influence.

We are told that "actions speak louder than words"; and proverbs are occasionally true. What is the appropriateness of jailing sundry misguided and usually harmless folks for preaching communism or anarchy, when we know perfectly well that every successful and well-to-do violator of the Volstead Act is a more efficacious agent of nihilism than a score of silly soap-box sputterers? When the intelligentsia picks and chooses which laws it will obey and which it will disregard, what is the proletariat to think of Law in general? "This statute about combinations in restraint of trade," says the burglar, "is a sensible one, and I heartily approve of it. Such combinations send up the price of tools. But as to that law in regard to breaking and entering with intent to commit a felony, I never had an opportunity to vote on it, I consider it an unjustifiable encroachment on individual freedom, and I shall manifest my contempt for it as often as I can." Many respected and respectable people have the same feeling toward our protective tariff. "A corrupt and infamous piece of legislation," they say, "one more honored in the breach than in the observance." And they so honor it whenever they return from Paris. Of course professional smuggling is quite a different matter. To be a blameless smuggler, one must maintain one's amateur status.

Yet there are bad laws, and so there will be, as long as the majority shall be fallible. What is a man to do in the presence of a law that he believes to be bad? That is one of the problems of Democracy. Ours is a crooked old world. It is only an oblate spheroid, anyhow; so modern geography tells us. Under the Ptolemaic system, when the earth was round, it was probably easier to see straight and to walk straight, and to keep to the strait path without misspelling it.

"Do right, and fear no man," sententiously observed the actor who was performing opposite Al Jolson at the Winter Garden. "I's got a better motto than that, Mr. Robinson," retorted the dusky star (in the rôle of Crusoe's Man Friday). "Don't write, and fear no woman."

A lady who was obliged to issue forth for an unexpected errand, her house remaining entirely devoid of inmates, deposited on the kitchen table this note for the provision man: "Gone out for two hours. Don't leave anything." On her return, she found the residence stripped of its silverware and other valuables, to the last ear-ring; and at the bottom of her kitchen table note was this addition: "Thank you, mum, we haven't."

Surely, the Winter Garden Man Friday and the burglarious author of the postscript were respecters of most of the conventions. They doubtless respected as many as you and I, though not exactly the same ones. For, as I said before, we are all ruled by habit. Strongest of all impulses is the gregarious instinct, which, we are told, will move a whole flock of sheep to throw itself over a precipice if its leader shall have accidentally tumbled there—so proving that the herd sentiment is more powerful than the instinct of self-preservation.

I know a man—Mr. Justin Wright—who regulates according to the gregarious calendar his whole life and, as far as possible, that of his friends. He is as good a man as you could find in a month of Sundays, but all his manifestations of goodness follow the lines of generally accepted precedent. Is a new book by Emil Ludwig in vogue? He reads it aloud to his family, who would undoubtedly appreciate it more if they were not dying to read one by Christopher Morley. Are the season and the weather appropriate for moonlight picnics? Off on a moonlight picnic all his guests must go, although they hate moonlight picnics considerably worse than sin, and he (to do him justice) hates these chilly outings just as much as they do. All his amusements are acts of self-abnegation, both for himself and for his beneficiaries. Such and such a game must be played, at such and such an hour, not because he likes it and not because his companions like it (for none of them do), but just because everybody likes it. Thus he overcomes his secret detestation of bridge, in which ostensible delectation Fate steadily afflicts him with incredibly and maddeningly poor hands. Even thus, in mute sacrifice of long afternoons that might have been spent on the mountain-tops, does he cultivate an overmastering enthusiasm for golf—a passion which, perhaps because of its insincerity, is evidently not returned by the cruelly coquettish game; for his scores never become one whit more conducive to truthfulness. Equally demonstrative is his appreciation of "pre-war" Scotch whiskey, which, although it invariably gives him a stomach-ache, he never fails to pronounce a sovereign remedy for all the ills of flesh or spirit. If he builds a cottage in a bleak and foggy summer resort, he buries it under a thicket of dank, dark trees, not because he is averse from sunlight and a worshiper of cold and dampness, but because the traditional holiday residence, being adapted to a hot season, traditionally seeks the shade.

"Thou shalt honor the Sabbath morning and keep thy golf for the afternoon." So the commandment now reads. Justin Wright's Sunday indignation at the man who plays in the forenoon is surpassed only by his resentment at the illiberal clergyman who would object to harmless sport in the postmeridian hours. We have traveled far from the Puritan days when Sunday began with Saturday's sunset. Moreover, the abridgment of the Sabbath has not resulted in concentration. No, Mr. Wright's Sunday has not been intensified by its reduction to a couple of hours. Church-going is optional; but ostentatious absenteeism is to be reprehended. To be seen playing tennis while the conformists were marching churchward would be unpardonable. On the other hand, automobiling, even during service time, is in the best of repute. A walk into the woods is a bit dubious; Mr. Wright is inclined to think it may be hazarded, but not in sporting clothes.

Speaking of clothes, how oddly things seem to balance one another, even in the scales of Fashion! Just as the female of the species has fairly adopted the sanest, scantiest, sightliest garb she has worn since the days of ancient Greece, what does the stupid male do but achieve the maximum of discomfort, superfluity, and ugliness with plus-fours and Oxford bags! I wonder which sex, in the annals of dress, has the record for absurdity. It is generally thought that each (and especially the deadlier) attires itself to attract the other. That seems to be true of some birds, but it will scarcely hold for human beings. "Human" is really no word to apply to some of the monstrosities which Fashion perpetrates. In the *Geographic Magazine* and elsewhere I have seen pictures of the womenfolk of some ultra-savage tribe who wear dinner-plates in their lips—that is, wedged into either lip, standing out horizontally and held in place by a narrow strip of flesh, a great wooden disk a foot or more in diameter, making the countenance resemble a grotesque nutcracker. Eating must be nearly impossible; speech quite so. The acquisition of such ornament, and the retention of it, must mean a life of unremitting agony. No one need tell me that a man, however benighted, wants his soul-mate to look like that. And no one need tell me that a woman, however Freudian, would submit to such torture to allure a man, even if she were sure the clattering dinner-plates possessed irresistible sex-appeal. No! only one power in the universe can command such sacrifice. And that power is Habit.

When women attire themselves, and when men do likewise, each sex no doubt has the other more or less in mind. Yet the all-compelling motive of each is not to fascinate the other, but to surpass its own kind in conformity to Habit. If love result, as a by-product, so much the better; the main output, however, is self-satisfaction, due to victory over one's peers. When Justin Wright for the first time dons a pair of plus-sixes, does he even momentarily flatter himself that ladies will deem him beautiful? No, the one and only mental picture that cheers him on is an image of the furious envy of his rival in conformity, Donald Keye, who has not yet advanced beyond plus-fours. When Baudelaire painted his hair green (if he ever did), was it done to ensnare and enslave wondering femininity? Never in the world! His one goal was the open-mouthed admiration of a little group of artists whose supreme Convention was Unconventionality. So when the Misses Wright daub their lips with nasty, ill-looking red paint, which makes them repellant to the eye and must make them (one conceives) still more repulsive to the taste, they are not seeking but renouncing masculine approbation, and all for that

Divinity whom the platter-mouthed negresses adore
—the Habit which we call Fashion.

I am always sorry for red-headed girls. Not that I
dislike red hair; on the contrary, I think it very
beautiful. Furthermore, red hair, which has always
appealed to artists, is now-a-days generally approved.
"Redhead" or "Redtop" or "Carrots" has ceased
to be an opprobrious epithet. The ruddy poll no
longer suggests Judas Iscariot; in this unbiblical age
it does not even recall Esau, who after all was not a
bad chap, although the Lord hated him and he was
no match for his twin brother, Jakey. I am sorry for
them because they never can paint themselves otherwise than discordantly. The palette of the beauty
parlor contains no red that does not swear with the
hue of their locks. Lips, cheeks, and hair, which
ought to agree like birds in their little nest, dwell in
shrieking cacophony. There would seem to be no
help for it, unless the auriferous damsels should
adapt Baudelaire's policy and paint their cheeks and
lips green.

A French comic paper recently had a picture of
two ultra-modern flappers standing at the doorway
of a drawing-room and gazing rapturously in at a
man—a very tall, abnormally thin and hollow-
chested man, with a perfectly bald head and a big
mustache; and flapper number one is saying ruefully
to flapper number two: "Ah! if we could only look
exactly like him!"

After all, dress is not the most important of habits, easiest though it be to philosophize about. There is the habit of going on a lark, a habit so exacting that it often exceeds the courage of the practitioner. "Where are you bound for, Seth?" said Ezry, meeting a friend at the railway station in Bangor. "I'm goin' to Augusty to have a reg'lar good old drunk," replied Seth, "and, my Gawd! how I dread it!"

One evening I was sitting alone in a *café* at Saint-Malo. It was a big *café*, used for concerts, and attached to the Hôtel Chateaubriand et de l'Europe. On the platform a lady orchestra was performing popular airs. There was a long printed list of tunes, numbered; and people in the audience had the privilege (seldom exercised) of calling by number for a tune they desired. Approaching my solitude I observed two middle-aged Englishmen, who, despite their unmistakable air of general decorum were evidently out for a devil of a time. One looked a little like Asquith, the other made me think of the Captain in one of Trollope's novels. No table was entirely vacant; mine had two empty seats. A brief whispered colloquy ensued between the two sports; then one of them, flushing violently, spoke: "I beg your pardon, sir, would you mind if we sat at your table?" Not in the least. Seated, and provided with small drinks, they carried on a conversation which might have been more successfully diabolic had it not been for a nervous consciousness that a stranger was overhearing. And yet I made myself as far away as possible; indeed, after a little I had almost forgotten them. Suddenly I was recalled by a gleeful chuckling and cries of "By Jove, we will!" "This time, no funking!" "Number three it is." Then, evidently appalled at their audacity but determined to put it through, whatever it was, the Captain rapped with his cane on the metal table and the Statesman held up three fingers, trembling but triumphant. Obediently the lady orchestra commenced the prelude to number three, which turned out to be a now forgotten masterpiece entitled, I believe, *Yip-i-Yaddy*. The guilty twain turned rather pale and cleared their throats. Then, after several inquiring glances to and fro, the Captain turned to me, scarlet with confusion: "Pardon me, sir, but I say, you know, won't you sing with us? We'd jolly well like to have you, if you're willin'? You see," he faltered, "we've called for number three, and we're goin' to sing the chorus. We tried it last night, but it somehow went wrong. It's sure to go better tonight. It will be a jolly good lark. '*Yip-i-Yaddy*', you know." "I am ashamed to say," was my reply, "that I do not know '*Yip-i-Yaddy*.' I have been living for some time on the Continent," I added apologetically. "Never mind!" they cried eagerly, "we'll teach it to you. Now listen!" And with a solemn schoolroom intonation the Statesman dictated something to this effect: "'Yip-i-Yaddy, i-ay, i-ay, Yip-i-Yaddy, i-ay, I don't care what the

words may be, if only you'll warble that sweet melo-
dee, Yip-i-Yaddy, i-ay, i-ay, Yip-i-Yaddy, i-ay.' Do
you think you've got it sir?" So anxious did he look
that I hastened to reassure him. By this time I had
also caught the tune, such as it was. The orchestra
had apparently played a couple of strophes and
was about to begin on the second round of the refrain.
Three mouths opened, and from one of them came a
sound of perceptible volume, while from the orifices
of the Statesman and the Captain issued the belief
of a tune. I am told that a violin string, without the
wood, can be heard only a foot and a half away. So it
was with the voices of the sporty couple. Anyhow,
they had the firm and exultant conviction that they
were singing. And thus it came to pass that I enter-
tained the Café Chateaubriand et de l'Europe with a
solo rendering of *Yip-i-Yaddy*, and that two English
gentlemen were made unspeakably happy with the
sense of sin.

I have never seen the two warblers since then, but
I have often thought of them and wondered to what
walk of life they belonged. It is hard for an American
to judge correctly the social status of a casual Englishman; almost always the rating is too high. For one
thing, the stranger is apt to be goodlooking and carefully dressed. Then there are his condescending
intonations. And, most important of all, he speaks
our common language so much more neatly than
we do.

Mr. Isaac Fiedelheimer, having spent thirty-five years in New York and made a pile of money, made also the discovery that his East Side accent, which no striving could diminish, was a bar to his social advancement. His son Percival must have a better chance. With this end in view, he conducted the lad to Coldspring College, one September morn, and presented him to the Dean, who had an almost national repute as a master of elegant diction—Dean Ethelred Fitzgibbon, sometimes even taken for an Englishman. "I vant my boy to go to your colletch," explained the father, "and I vant him to lif in your house until he loins to talk goot English like you do." The Dean's face was cold and hard. "I vill pay anyting you ask," pleaded the fond father. The Dean's countenance registered only haughty annoyance. "And I vill gif de colletch tventy tousant dollars." The Dean's expression changed. Perhaps, after all, for the sake of the old College, it was his duty to accept the offer. Besides, who knew what might be made of the young man? When examined sympathetically, he really had an uncommonly capable look. The following June, when Mr. Fiedelheimer returned to fetch his offspring, the Dean stared at him in blank unrecognition. "Don't you know me?" Only a shrug was the Dean's reply, his hands, palm upward, elevated shoulder-high, and a downward trend in the corners of his mouth. "Vy, I'm Fiedelheimer," cried the astonished parent. "O my Got, Mr. Fiedelheimer," exclaimed the Dean, "for vy didn't I know you? Egscuse me. Listen! Come in and see vat ve haf loined your boy. And don't forget vat you set about de tventy tousant."

We all want our children to be different from our-selves, and to speak a different lingo. "My daughter's doin' all right, thank you," answered a Yankee villager. "No, she ain't teachin' school this year. You know she used to teach French. Well, she got all the French she could out o' books, an' now she's spendin' a year in Paris to git the twang." The twang is the thing. Educating one's family in Europe, to be sure, is a pretty expensive habit, though a very ancient one. Older than you think, perhaps. Consider the case of Judge Ibzan, in Judges xii, 8 and 9; "And after him Ibzan of Beth-le-hem judged Israel. And he had thirty sons and thirty daughters, whom he sent abroad." Think of doing that on a judge's salary! Such is the power of Habit.

SYMPATHY

No charges can approximate
The worth of sympathy with woe
(Although I think I ought to state
He did his best to make them so).

THUS sang Gilbert of Barnes Carew, the sympathetic
lawyer. This poor old world gets a plenty of hard
knocks, and generally deserves them. But there is one
amiable quality for which, though we all know our
globe possesses it almost in superabundance, the
credit given is always insufficient: I mean—as the
intelligent reader may have guessed from my title,
my quotation, and my opening sentence—the quality
of sympathy.

I have calculated that of my daily mail throughout
the year 99.99 per cent. postulates the assumption that
I am all heart; for it consists of petitions—requests for
money, for labor, for recommendations, with no
conceivable chance of return. Now I readily confess
that I am nearly all heart (like most of the people I
know), but I am partly stomach, too, and have to
devote small portions of my time and my earnings to
the satisfaction of that organ.

The business of recommendations alone might, if
properly done, fill a forty-eight-hour week. To make

the most appetizing case for the applicant without
actually lying to the overfed employer, and to do it in
terms sufficiently individual to stamp an impression,
and a different impression every time—that is art;
and art, Hippocrates has told us, is long, compared to
the brevity of human life. The basic principle of
recommending, as of theoretically correct advertising
(so I am told), is to tell the truth and nothing but the
truth, but not the whole truth. If you are boosting a
brand of matches, you may declare that they will
light on nothing but the box and are therefore safe
playthings for mice; but you need not add that they
never light on anything at all without breaking in
two. Are you advocating the candidacy of a prospec-
tive teacher? He is industrious, you rightly affirm, a
youth of excellent Christian character, a student of
high rank; but are you called upon to prophesy that
he will never set the Thames on fire?

Then there are the promises you have to make to
espouse the cause of sundry decent but chronically
incompetent persons, "should a suitable opportunity
occur." You really are sure you could do it in a
minute, under the conditions stated; at the bottom
of your heart, however, you know very well that no
opportunity within the compass of your imagination
can ever be made to appear "suitable." Perhaps it
would be kinder, in the long run, to tell the poor
devil frankly that there is no chance for him. Yet he
means awfully well, he has a family to support, and

he would presumably be just as bad at one thing as
another. Must he be deprived of hope? Besides, once
in a dog's age the unexpected does happen; and then
it is hard to tell which is the happier, the deserving
and long-suffering office-seeker or the long-suffering
and not-very-deserving benefactor, who, by some
strange caprice of fortune, has finally landed his
client in a job.

I wonder whether I should have done better to
refrain from answering the first epistle sent me, three
or four years ago, by an unknown crazy woman somewhere in Ohio. It was a very long letter, on fool's cap
paper, requiring eight cents' postage. Doubtless she
she had got my name out of some catalog; and I dare
say she has mailed similar communications to other
strangers in various parts of the country. She is compelled to write, she avers, because she has something
of supreme importance to tell me—nothing less than
a message for me from Mars (I mean the planet, not
the God of War). Though a poor, ignorant person,
she continues, she has succeeded in putting herself in
harmony with the Cosmic Vibrations, and has thus
become a receiving apparatus for the Thought of the
Universe. Furthermore, she has discovered that I am
one of the few elect on earth who have the power to
become Cosmic Receivers, will they but try. Some
general directions follow for achieving such Receiver-
ship, and some friendly urging to begin my attempt
at once. Then come many, many, many pages of

Cosmic Vibrations, symbolized by all manner of little curved lines, half an inch or so long, arranged in rows according to a system revealed to her. It does not look at all like a language, either alphabetic or ideographic. But it conveys the vibrated and vibrant message of Mars to me. What that message is, I still apprehend but vaguely. Naturally I returned a polite answer, thanking her for her kind interest in a total stranger and for the great pains she had been at. Indeed, the labor of executing all these quirks with pen and ink must have been very considerable. Since that time, at quarterly intervals, I have been receiving the sequel—long, chubby, eight-cent envelopes stuffed with Cosmic Vibrations. By this time, I know these envelopes as soon as I see them, for I recognize the sprawling, ingenuous hand of the writer. I am sure the poor woman derives real pleasure—perhaps her only pleasure—from her vibratory experiences. I never responded again. Ought I to have kept on answering her, or ought I never to have answered at all?

Many of the petitions one receives from strangers (and even from friends) are about as wild as the adjurations of the Cosmic Receiver. I suppose it is the same with anybody whose name is readily accessible. One never would have believed that the whole material, spiritual, and imaginary universe contained so much utterly valueless information as that which is annually called for by inquiring correspondents. For

instance, a lady once asked who it was that made the
dedicatory speech at the inauguration of a statue of
some local celebrity in a small town in Italy several
years before. I did look that up, because I knew and
esteemed the lady; it meant half a day in the Public
Library with files of Italian newspapers. But why she,
who had no particular interest in Italy, should have
sought this special crumb of knowledge, I have
never found out. Many of the things craved are
simply unobtainable; others might perhaps be dug
up if one had nothing else to do. None, or virtually
none, have anything to do with me. Two men in
Texas have made a bet about the population of
Missouri in 1886. A student in the University of
Oklahoma, who is writing a thesis on Booth Tarking-
ton, inquires how many copies of that author's books
are to be found in the public libraries of New England
and how often each one of them is taken out in the
course of a year. I know none of the answers; and
I should not be a whit happier or wiser if I knew
them all.

Even more numerous than pleas for information
are appeals for money. On the average, there are
about three a day all through the twelvemonth. And
I am counting only the good ones; only the charities
that pull at your heartstrings, and only the societies,
magazines, and journals that seem to be of some real
use. For alas! societies and publications spring up
mushroom-like overnight, by the dozens, by the

scores; and only a few can justify their existence. We have a mania for organizing. Highly specialized groups are formed to differentiate the work of bigger associations, while large-scale agglomerations are planned to coördinate the activities of existing societies. Then there are surveys and questionnaires and chain letters. Always more and more machinery, and, in proportion to the outlay, less and less result.

I do not complain of these things. Everybody has his troubles, and mine are doubtless no worse than other people's; indeed, fellow-creatures better endowed with money or with information must, I suppose, be mulcted far more heavily than I. No, I cite these varied and numerous supplications simply as proofs of man's confidence in man—of the universal faith in human sympathy.

Incomparably the most frequent attack upon one's ingenuous sensibilities is the entreaty to buy something, either something of no conceivable utility or something possibly usable but inflatedly dear. That is the appeal which we call advertising. Although the whole epistolary mass of it, or very nearly the whole, goes, with its message all unspoken, straight into the ash-can, it affords additional evidence—portentous in its bulk and pathetic in its futility—of the same beautiful faith I am extolling.

Happily that belief, though too all-embracing to be fully realized, has a solid foundation in human nature. Evidences thereof fill even the most trivial

occurrences of our daily lives. Mrs. Malaprop, kindly
interested in the reviving health of her sick neighbor,
Mrs. Languish, meets on the street the village physician. "Oh! doctor," she cries, "I'm so glad to see that
you've stopped calling on Mrs. Languish; now I
know she's out of danger."

The Hon. Croesus Cashman, the multimillionaire,
has just engaged a room at a New York hotel. It is
luncheon time, and he is hungry; but alas! his diet is
severely restricted, his wealth having been won at the
expense of his digestion. Sadly he opens his suit-case
and draws therefrom a package of those crisp biscuits
known as "educators," and sends a colored porter
out to fetch him a pint of milk. Then and there, in the
privacy of his room, he begins his joyless repast. The
porter lingers, gazing compassionately. The longer
he looks, the more intense his suffering. At last he can
endure the pitiful sight no more. "Say, boss, you
needn't eat dat stuff. Right in de nex' block I can tell
you a place where you can get a fust-rate chicken
dinner wid watermillion, for thirty-five cents."

Speaking of the kindliness of the lowly, I once had a
feline member of the household, Sneezer by name, a
devoted retainer, all gentleness and affection for the
family, a tigress in defence of her frequently recurring
kittens. As I returned to my house one day, I found,
to my consternation, extended across my front steps
a huge strange dog. There it lay, sprawling and de-
fiant, entirely blocking my path, an ugly beast. I am

sure it was as big as an undersized pony. "Go home, doggy!" said I, with an affectation of friendly conde- scension. "Grrrr," answered the intruder. "Go home!" I then commanded, my extended arm pointing towards its supposed domicile. "Grrrrrr" was the only reply that issued from the shark-like jaws. I had no weapon, not even an umbrella, Discretion was evidently the better course. "Pretty doggy!" I ven- tured. This overture met with no appreciation; "grrr, grrrr," remarked the savage animal, with an air unmistakably threatening. What was one to do? I must either give up my beloved home or straddle over the monstrous form. Just then I espied a head peering around the back corner of the house. It was the head of Sneezer, my faithful cat. On her mobile features was an expression of sympathy for my plight, mingled with dire suspicion of the stranger's motives in approaching the abode of her young. There was no time for further observation. Shooting through the air, as if expelled from a catupult, went a great yellow blur of caninity, emitting, as it sped, an un- broken series of agonized yelps; and Sneezer soared at its tail. Over the wall they flew, out and away into the world. Little by little the shrieks died away in the distance. Yet cynics say cats have no souls.

What a cruel thing is sympathy unrequited! "Good mornin', ma'am," cried with beaming face the friendly fruitman. "How about that melon, the extra big one I left last week? Did it do for the whole family?"

"Pretty nearly," answered the grim housewife. "The doctor is still calling."

On the other hand, if rightly fostered, sympathy can make heroes of us all. It made heroes of me and my colleague, Puffer. This episode, which may be called the Tale of Two Cities, occurred at a time when most of the people now alive were still waiting to be born. In those days the Charles River, between Boston and Cambridge, was as yet unimproved; but improvement was in sight, for preparations were afoot for the erection of the Harvard Bridge. Symptomatic of the age is the admiration with which we simple folk then regarded that lamentable structure, a marvel (it seemed to us) of power and grace.

To understand such a feeling, one must be familiar with what had gone before; and that can never be conceived by one who has not seen and smelt it. No wonder the sun so often veiled its face. The bridge (the old bridge), on which the poet stood at midnight, appeared at its best at that hour—or, I should say, an hour earlier, before the moon had risen over the city. Nothing but a causeway with a draw in the middle, it was saved from criticism by its lack of pretentions. Cambridge's only communication with Boston, or (as a Cantabrigian would put it) Boston's only communication with Cambridge, was afforded by that causeway and interrupted by that draw. Frequent and long were the interruptions. Judging from them, one would have inferred an almost ceaseless flood of commerce surging to and fro on the river; whereas all that one could actually see in the course of a day was a half-dozen scows, a tug, and a barge or two. My own theory is that the draw-keeper had other functions, perhaps in distant parts of the city; having once opened the passage, he would put it out of his mind and turn his thoughts and steps to some remoter and doubtless more important duty. Meanwhile continuity lay broken and the two cities could only gaze wistfully at each other like Hero and Leander, from far-off shores. "Traffic" (as we had not yet learned to call it) was divided, not Gallic-wise into three parts, but into two. Little by little a long line of carts, drays, carriages, and pedestrians would collect on either side, and, at the end of each procession, a little red horse-car. Then happened what eventually did happen every time: the keeper returned, the Hellespont was closed, the opposing caravans once more made contact, and the stream grew together again like the segments of a severed snake.

The above-mentioned little red horse-cars were our rapid transit. (One of my contemporaries says "green," another says "yellow": I therefore stick to red.) Between Harvard Square in Cambridge and Bowdoin Square in Boston they laboriously plodded, generally stuffed to the bursting-point with aging passengers. In winter-time a pitchforkfull of hay on the floor was their sole luxury. At all seasons, but oftenest in the cold ones (autumn, winter, and

spring), the vehicle, during its transit, would contrive
to leave the rails and run bumpety-bump over the
cobble-stones, shaking out the travelers' boughten
teeth and seating ladies and gentlemen with gay
promiscuity in one another's laps. Sometimes this
welcome interlude would continue for several blocks.
In many cases, indeed, the track was not regained
until a halt had been called, all passengers ordered
outside, and the stoutest and boldest of them had lent
a hand in lifting the car back to its lost pathway.
Impatient youths, vowing that it was shorter to walk,
would relinquish the benefit of their fares and entrust
themselves to their unaided legs. But it did them no
good in the long run; the car would always overhaul
them at the draw.

As to the river, you must remember that in the
antiquity whereof I speak it really was a river, and
not a stone tank. That is, of course, a tide-river, for the
tides "still rolled in the bay as they rolled that day
when the Mayflower moored below." When they
rolled out, they left on either hand a wide, black
margin of mud, slime, tins, cats, vegetables, discarded
clothing, and miscellaneous refuse, saturated with
sewage from the Boston shore. Nobody ever dared
cross the bridge, at low tide, with both arms full of
packages, because one hand was needed to hold one's
nose. Like a sandstorm in the desert, the stench would
come surging on, and horrid death was the penalty
for unprotected nostrils. And so it seemed destined to

remain forever. What a long, hard fight the advocates of "improvement" had to make, before ancient rights and prejudices could be worsted! The crux of the matter lay in the disposal of the Back Bay drainage— the diversion of it from the river into a sewer. How the Beacon Streeters did kick against the pricks, stoutly maintaining until the final gasp that their aristocratic sewage exhaled no offensive odor! At last the proletariat won, the Beacon St. drainage flowed through Beacon St. By that time, to be sure, the Blue Blood of the Back Bay had been considerably thinned by recent extraneous admixture.

Well, at the date of my story the New Harvard Bridge, a good piece above the causeway, was actually started, but the cleaning-up process was still in the blue-print stage. Of course, such a startling enterprise as a New Bridge (a real bridge, too, not just a causeway) created a considerable flutter, especially on the Cambridge side; and many visitors came to inspect the preparations. Among the sightseers, one afternoon, were Puffer and I, youthful colleagues at Harvard. Puffer was a man in whose build the three dimensions had attained quasi-equality. In character, moreover, he was four-square. His face was at once revelatory and deceptive; for while his big black beard betrayed his romantic temperament, it belied his fundamental gentleness; and his great round glasses, though indicative of erudition, conveyed no suggestion of adventurousness. Yet, the spirit of adventure it was, the itch for the unknown, which led him, and dragged me, into the perilous situation which furnishes the plot of this narrative.

At this point the reader, however gentle habitually, may begin to evince impatience, complaining that of the plot just alleged he has perceived not a trace, all the foregoing paragraphs having been devoted to "atmosphere"—and none too appetizing atmosphere, at that. Let him, I beg, forbear a little longer, remembering the sensationally emotional character of the tale, and remembering also that in bloodcurdlers the background counts for at least three-quarters of the effect. Let him now picture to himself a scene of primitive foul desolation upon which the nineteenth century, in the form of sundry heaps of piles and planks, is just beginning to intrude—a wide expanse of sticky, stinky black mud, curving, like a titanic finger-nail, around a none too clean giant finger of Cambridge shore.

What demon of inquisitiveness pushed Puffer and me further and further out over the flats? Further and further afield we wandered, each following his own nose, intent on his own investigations (whatever they may have been), until I was suddenly arrested by a cry of distress from my companion, who, as usual, was in the lead. As I approached him he appeared to me curiously reduced or distorted, the exact balance of his three dimensions being disturbed either by a strange diminution of length or by a still stranger increase of breadth and thickness. Haste was made impossible by the stickiness of the soil, which, as I advanced, grew more and more yielding and adhesive. Every time I pulled up my foot, the movement produced a sound like the uncorking of a bottle; and I observed that, despite my eagerness to proceed, the intervals between these discharges became disquietingly longer and longer. Inspecting Puffer at closer range, I discovered that the disproportion between length and the other two dimensions had slightly but unmistakably increased; and I convinced myself that it was due to the subsidence of the lower part of his legs, which were gradually sinking into the mud. Occasional efforts to wriggle himself loose only accelerated the rate of absorption. For the most part, indeed, he remained stoically calm, like Farinata degli Uberti erect in his fiery tomb and "holding Hell in great contempt"; but from time to time, even as a half-exhausted fly netted in the spider's web, he would make for a moment a desperate struggle. Each such attempt sent him a little further down. Once—I shudder to relate it!—he tried to pry himself up with his hands; whereupon, as might have been expected, his arms sunk inextricably, and he stood fast planted on all fours, like a wooden ox from Noah's Ark. At the same moment his hat (a new bowler) pitched forward into the mire.

"Go back!" he commanded, as soon as he became aware of my proximity. "Save yourself! This is a

quicksand. I am doomed. Save yourself while you
may!'' These words of sublime altruism fired my
sympathy to a hitherto unknown pitch of self-
sacrifice. "Never!" I cried, "I will pull you out or
perish with you!" The energy with which I pronounced this phrase sent my hat to join Puffer's in the
ooze. "No!" he protested. "It is useless. One life is
enough. Save yourself, and bear the sad news home."
Then, with a great tear trickling down either cheek,
he entrusted to me a last message to his young wife,
and told me what disposal should be made of his
most cherished possessions. His unpublished epic
poem he bequeathed to me. This was too much.
With smaller tears than his, but rapider, coursing
over my visage and saltily into my mouth, I laid hold
of him. A difficult thing to do, because of his quad-
rupedal position. Wrenching his arms free, I seized
him by the armpits, wildly hoping with one Herculean
heave to lift him out. Alas! he was much heavier than
I. Instead of elevating him I found myself swiftly
descending to his level. Such is the history of many
an uplift movement. Just in the nick of time, by an
adroit spring I released Puffer and threw myself at
full length flat on my back.

As I lay there, I meditated, Puffer meanwhile
repeating his exhortations to abandon him to his
fate. Each full of sympathy for the other, we both
wept—I, couched in comfort on the slowly yielding
surface; he, firmly entrenched in the four-footed

posture which he had involuntarily resumed. But I had no idea of forsaking Puffer—no more than Pylades would desert Orestes, nor Orestes desert Pylades, when (in Pacuvius's tragedy) they both stood before the cruel Aegisthus, each clamoring to be the victim. Violence, however, had failed; I must use strategy. Scanning the horizon from my horizontal bed, I discovered, in four directions, though not far away, four boards of considerable size. Cautiously —very cautiously and not without difficulty—I rose to my feet. Then, without a word, I carried these timbers one by one, close to the still expostulating Puffer, who (as I observed with satisfaction) had apparently ceased to subside. There I built of them a little platform, standing on which, with renewed courage and renewed strength, grabbing my colleague once more under the arms, I succeeded in hoisting him into safety.

Face to face, hand clasping hand, erect on our tiny raft, we beamed upon one another like shipwrecked mariners with a rescuing sail in sight. Need I add that the tears, thick and hot, flowed down both countenances? Puffer's copious beard, in fact, was by this time quite saturated. A suitable period of time was given to regaining our composure. It would doubtless have been a longer period, had we not become aware that the raft which supported us was already lost to sight, being submerged to the extent of an inch or so. With dainty movements, and with footsteps as light as our natural heft and our recent accretions would allow, we made our way to *terra firma*. This, however, was not the end. Danger was past, but trouble was still ahead. There we were, three miles from home, in broad though waning daylight, in what condition you can imagine. We had, indeed, with commendable presence of mind, salvaged our hats—but oh! how changed! Our way lay through the middle of the thickly populated city. For Cambridge, even then, was a city of respectable size, whatever envious neighbors might say. With pride I record the fact that on this occasion we did not weep—neither Puffer nor I. Like the heroes we were, we simply put our heads together (metaphorically), and laid out a course. Each told the other all the dark alleys and disreputable back streets he could remember; and, combining our topographical resources, we contrived a route sufficiently obscure and sufficiently devious to avert arrest and to postpone arrival until dusk. And so it worked out. The police took no notice, not a dog bit us (although several barked indignantly), even the small boys of the meanest quarter respected our sorrow; and we reached home after dark.

FOG

It was a dense fog, but low. Although soft sunlight filtered through it, you were all alone in the world, if, like me, you were out in a canoe. The rest of the universe was quite obliterated. There was scarcely enough breeze to steer by, but I had a compass in my pocket, to use if need should arise. Besides, I knew every rock and every nook along that coast, every boat that lay at her mooring for a mile each way. Except for the short range of vision, it was like the streets I traverse daily to and fro, in the routine of business.

Yet all at once there sprang up before me something that had never been there before. A long way off it arose, bathed in misty brightness—a mountainous, rocky island, not unlike Capri, speckled with great white villas. Had some good enchanter magically transported me to another hemisphere, where Maxfield Parrish reigned, a land where "it seemed always afternoon"? If it had lasted only a moment, one might have explained the vision as an illusion. But it did not fade away as I approached; no, on the contrary, it rapidly grew. Higher the mountains rose, further stretched the rocky shore, bigger and closer clustered the gleaming mansions. Indeed, these villas seemed big out of all proportion to the island itself—a wild and barren country, apparently incapable of supporting even a small population, although a brownish growth covered its lower reaches.

Suddenly the scene changed, and completely. A few yards from my prow lay a reef, an old, familiar reef, at this tide some seventy feet long and six feet high, covered with white gulls. That was all. Never on the stage had I seen a transformation so perfect. Vanished was the new-world Capri, with its still, shining country-houses, its mountains, and its mystery. Yet not altogether gone, for the magic island has painted itself in my memory. It returns to my sight whenever I approach that reef; and at other times, too, when there is no material stimulus to suggest it. It has joined my collection of dream landscapes and dream houses—those places just as real as daylight objects, but usually seen in sleep.

For years and years there was a mountain (such a satisfactory mountain!), all glittering rock with bare, bold, rugged sides and a sharp peak, which used to appear to me in dreamland but nowhere else. You may guess how very fond I became of its crags and ravines, how familiar with its every contour; for I always saw it from the same point of view, except once, when I climbed it. At last, late one afternoon, four years ago, a miracle occurred: I saw that mountain projected into that part of reality which we call

waking. There it was at last, just as I had so often
seen it in my slumber! I was lying off Gibraltar,
looking at the African shore; and there it stood glistening, a great jagged hump of silver, the Monkey
Mountain. My dreams had come true.

Not often, with us prosaic people, does dream
become real, or reality become dreamlike. That is the
business of poets. A great poet may be likened to a
dream, which seems to create something beautiful
out of nothing at all; but every genuine poet is a fog,
transforming the ordinary into the marvelous. Dreams
of course are in fact made of something, but their
matter is so lost in the transmuting that we can seldom
detect it. The fog treatment frequently allows its
processes to be tracked; it attains its effects mainly by
shifting the near to a great distance; and we all know
what it is that distance lends to the view. Like fog,
and like the poet, distance conceals the ugly and
uninteresting parts, allowing only the attractive,
salient features to be seen. Everyday things become
alluring in proportion to their remoteness in time and
space. The castles on the Rhine had nothing romantic
for the people who built and used them; India is for
its British official residents a prosy enough affair—
unless they happen to be poets.

Poets, I suppose, are not likely to get such berths.
What is appreciated in a candidate for such a job is
efficiency, and this demands a scientific spirit. The
teacher of Roman History (that was before the New

Method, which combines all histories into one) was
holding forth on the sturdiness of the ancient stock.
"Think of this, boys," she said. "When Publius
Humidus Piscator was Consul he used every day to
swim three times across the Tiber before breakfast.
Three times every day . . . Well, Johnny, what
are you smiling at? Do you think it impossible to
swim across the Tiber three times?" "It ain't that,
ma'am," responded the youthful skeptic. "I was just
wonderin' how he got back to where his clothes
was." There speaks the scientific mind. Would a poet
ever have thought of that objection?

"When I was your age," observed Charley's great-
aunt, "I knew the names of all the Presidents of the
United States in order." "That's not so much,"
retorted Charley. "They wasn't very many Presidents then." Again the soulless scientist. "One drop
of this poison on a cat's tongue," cried the scientific
lecturer, "will kill a strong man." Even so does a
single drop of unsympathetic criticism kill the poet.
Preciseness, not preciousness, is what science demands. "The pain is in my stomach," declared the
250-pound patient, pathetically. The doctor gazed
rather hopelessly at the expanse in question. "Can't
you be a little more definite?" he asked. The utter-
most of precision is of course to be sought in numbers.
"This chair," said the amateur antiquary, "must be a
good hundred years old; for I saw Auntie Elder sit
in it twenty years ago, and she was over eighty." The

statistician is really the man who rocks the world's
cradle. Not long ago I read in an article in *The
Nation*: "The figures as they stand on their face are
staggering." If you are poet enough, try to visualize
the scene. I dare say, though, a poet is the only kind
of man that can stand on his face without staggering;
for topsy-turvy is the poet's equilibrium.

"Is there any profit in poetry?" asked the matter-
of-fact friend. "Why, surely," replied the bard. "Only
this last week I sent two poems to the editor and got
three back." Thus does the poet cast his bread upon
the waters. Why expect him to be practical? Is there
profit in dreams (unless you are a psycho-analyst)?
Or in fog?

A curious thing about fog is that when it thoroughly
envelops you, barring out the rest of the world, you
have an intensely strong sense of direction; and it is
always wrong. Of nothing whatever are you so certain in the fogless stretches of your life. You may
hesitate a moment when asked your age. I once
knew a man—a very able man of forty or thereabouts
—who could not remember his own name when
suddenly questioned by an official in a bank. He had
to go out and walk up and down the street several
times before he could make the connection. Yet I
venture to say that, if he were caught in a dense fog,
with nothing to indicate north or south, he would be
as sure of his points as a Fundamentalist is sure of
Hell. Bring out the compass and show him that his

directions are all at sixes and sevens. "The compass must be out of order," he would answer confidently. Why is it that under such circumstances we become absolutely devoid of common sense? Does the fog make poets of us all? Or is it always the case that the firmness of our convictions is in inverse proportion to the evidence? Total absence of proof would then naturally result in perfect certainty. That sounds plausible, when we consider the opinions of our friends. And, inasmuch as evidence is habitually scarce, the principle makes for self-assurance, and (it follows) for efficiency.

We inefficient literary folk are expected to look up with awe at the majestic heights of efficiency attained by business and by journalism. And—I hasten with breakneck speed to add—we generally do. Only once in an age does the presumptuous idea occur to us to judge by what we see, and not by what we are told. One thing in the world of affairs that we can always see, and cannot fail to see, is advertising. Now, of the advertisements which swell our newspapers, and which because of their multitude we never read, I shall say nothing. We are assured they obey certain mysterious laws beyond our comprehension. But we may venture to form an opinion about the matter that comes to us in envelopes, by mail. That opinion, an opinion amounting to a conviction, is that commercial houses never revise their mailing lists. You may move, you may change your name, you may die;

your address on the mailing list will remain unaltered. It does no good to write and tell the mailing clerk that you have removed, taken your rich uncle's name, or died; he never believes you. My father-in-law, for twenty years after his death, was pursued annually by the same notices from the same firms, although they had all been promptly and repeatedly notified. Fifteen years ago I ceased to be editor of a quarterly which I had directed for the ten years preceding. Every interested party was told; every number of the magazine bears the name and address of the present editor. Yet I venture to say the bulk of the purely business correspondence still comes to me and has to be forwarded. Fear not, O mortal, to sicken, perish, and be forgotten; you will live on, in the business mailing lists, until the Judgment Day. Then, awakened by the Last Trump, you will find yourself buried under a mountain of accumulated one-cent printed matter. Even as some of our great cities, on election day, summon their graveyards to the polls, so do our great commercial houses make their appeal to the unnumbered dead.

It really is useless to perish. That was the conclusion eventually reached by the Irishman who attempted suicide. Tired of life (and advertisements), he went all over his apartment, turned on all the gas jets, lighted them, and then sat down to die.

Concerning journalism we literary or semi-literary people have more information than we possess concerning Big Business. We know that it is founded on two principles: first, to mix news and advertisements beyond the power of disentangling; second, never to refer to anything that is twenty-four hours old. For rule number one, the reason is obvious. This is the plan: one captures the eye with scare headings, one begins as many things as possible on the front page and never finishes anything there, the purpose being, of course, to lure the reader into a jungle of advertisements. Instead of that, alas! thanks to the mental and physical gymnastics required for perusing inside layers, Mr. Common People never reads beyond the opening paragraph of anything, except the sporting columns—as you can easily ascertain by listening to the conversation of newspaper readers. They all know the age, name, and home address of the victim, but have not reached the probable criminal nor the real story of the crime.

For the second law of journalism—the twenty-four hour limit—I have never been able even to guess an effective cause. Take a scientific association; it may be doing things of the greatest benefit (or detriment) to society, but it cannot get space in the paper until there is an annual election of officers. Nobody cares a tinker's dam who the officers are, but they alone have the *entrée*. Journalists are possessed by an incomprehensible mania for proper names—a sadly misplaced affection, because orthographically the names always elude them. There is, let us say, a change of cabinet in Jugoslavia. No hint do we get of what the row is about, nothing but a list of the outgoing and incoming ministries, presumably misspelt beyond recognition—even assuming there were anyone in the country who had the interest to try. During the World War it was my duty to preside at a number of public meetings and to sit innocuous on the platform at a good many more. Always there was in front of us, on the floor, a long table for reporters. There they would sit, behind a jumble of papers, looking as important and as busy as a man can look who does nothing at all. Never, on any occasion, did I see one of them take a note during the performance. At the close, however, they would come rushing at us pell-mell, to secure the names and addresses of the platform-sitters. The object of the assembly was a matter of indifference; so were the speeches, unless some knowing Cicero should hand them a brief type-written summary of his own remarks. Then, if there happened to be a scarcity of murders and divorces, the fore-sighted orator might expect a little paragraph to himself—of course with his name misspelt. It is astounding how many possibilities there are in the way of cacography. Once, in the old days, a college paper (the *Harvard Echo*) announced that anyone might join the Bicycle Club "by singing the constitution." Here is a metathesis so simple and so effective that it seems inevitable; yet, as far as I can ascertain, it never found employment before. Enviable Bicycle Club, the home of harmony!

Can such concord prevail in any other sport—in golf, for instance?

A young lady was taking golf lessons from a professional. Her face brightened into smiles, for lo! an idea was born unto her. "I know now," she cried, "what is the trouble with my game! I stand too near the ball before I drive." "Not exactly, ma'am," replied the cold wisdom of the expert. "The trouble with you is, you stand too near the ball after you drive." Our distance from the ball after we drive; that is the measure of efficiency. A good theme for a homily; but I hasten on.

In academic life we lay small claim to efficiency. I have more than once been present at the forcible feeding of a baby. A fond mother supported the child in her arms; the father confined, as well as he could, its hands and feet; a maid held its nose, in order to compel the mouth to open for breath; while a trained nurse stood watchfully prepared to insert a spoonful of food as soon as the jaws should separate. Such was (and still is for the most part) the typical American college; an expert body of administrators whose business it is to hold the student's hands, feet, and nose, while the agile professor injects a few drops of vital sustenance. That is why, in our academic communities, the Administration Building looms up so big. The American traveler observes with amazement that European institutions of higher learning have no Administration Building. They need none, because they have virtually no administration. In fact, if our colleges were what they purport to be,—academies whose function is to provide eager youth with an opportunity to profit by the lessons of mature knowledge,—what administration would be needed, beyond the services of a competent janitor?

It is not entirely presumptuous ignorance that moves me to criticism; for I once had a curious experience as administrator—enough to give me a glimpse of the inside of the routine. I was twenty-six years old, and had been teaching for three years. When summer came, the excellent Secretary of the College, who had been working long and hard without respite, felt the need of a considerable vacation, and asked me to take his place during the months of closure. Accordingly I was installed as Acting Secretary, with a desk in the deserted Faculty room. Every morning early I left my seaside quarters and betook myself to that improvised office. And every morning, as I entered the College precincts by the same gate, the same boy, with the same badge declaring him an Authorized Guide, would hail me and offer to show me the College buildings. His persistence I admired as much as I mourned its futility. I had to comfort myself with the thought that perhaps he did occasionally find a responsive stranger. It was a lonely place, though. In those days there was no summer school. At first, other and greater officials were with me for a part of the day; but presently the

Dean departed, then the Registrar, next the untitled lady who kept the records and was therefore regarded by studentdom as the real manager of the show; at last the President, and, a few days later, his private secretary. Alone, at twenty-six, in the great College. Nevertheless, I had no time for solitary brooding. Visitors were continually dropping in and there was a constant flow of correspondence; and both callers and letters were full of questions—some trifling, some important—for which I had to improvise answers, there being nobody to consult and my instructions being scanty.

My first business, of course, was to learn all the ropes. In the process I unearthed many interesting secrets—which I am not going to divulge, mainly because I have forgotten them. Speaking of secrecy, however, I discovered and shall reveal one typical fact: that a certain highly essential and complicated set of rules, which every instructor and every student really needed to know, existed in only one much folded, much soiled, and almost illegible copy, in a forgotten drawer of my desk. Nobody knew these rules, save the Secretary and the Dean, and they knew them by oral tradition alone. My principal service to the institution, during my incumbency, was to cause a great quantity of copies of this document to be printed, ready for distribution in the autumn. I am almost inclined to boast that this bold act of mine was a first step in the dissipation of that dense mystery which had previously enshrouded college offices. After that, the fog began to lift, to the detriment of poetry, perhaps, but surely to the advantage of education.

I wish I could remember all my visitors and the strange things that some of them wanted. One father, I recall, was determined that his boy should enter college, although the luckless son had persistently failed, year after year, in every one of his admission examinations. Of course there were very many such fathers and very many such sons. It was amazing how many failed when conditions were so easy that failure seemed impossible. This particular parent stands out in my memory because of his indefatigable resourcefulness. "There must be some way in which this matter can be arranged," he declared at last. "I am willing to spend unlimited effort—and unlimited money," he added (*avec intention*, as the stage directtions say in French plays). He had the air of an exceedingly prosperous business man. Ignoring the implication, I suggested the status of "special student." No, the boy must be a "regular" or nothing. Next I suggested a tutor. "I've tried them," was the reply. "Tutor after tutor. All no good. They try to teach things, but they don't teach the answers to the questions that are asked. Now, wouldn't it be possible for my boy to be tutored by the persons who make or mark the examinations?" And he looked at me with searching eyes. "That is not permitted," said I.

Steadily and hard he stared at me, while his face darkened. He was evidently not used to successful opposition. I nerved myself for an angry scene. After a long interval he spoke, wonderingly: "The more I see of your College, the more I respect it." And he quietly took his departure.

Back to my mind comes a long letter written by a youthful culprit in palliation of some offense of which he had been found guilty. It was a most intricate and ingenious story, and it closed with these words: "Mr. Secretary, I write this with an honest tongue." Somehow, there is a dash of poetry in that phrase.

But I must not forget the poet, the real poet, who came to see me one foggy day, having walked all the way from a little town in Ohio. He had heard of our college, he said, in his remote home; and he wanted to be a student.

He was only sixteen, two years younger than Marchbanks in *Candida*. And he looked incredibly like the poet of popular imagining: long brown hair; a pretty, childish face, but very earnest; a flowing tie, an ancient velvet waistcoat, trousers a bit short, cowhide boots. With modest confidence he drew from his pocket some specimens of his art. They were not half bad, it seemed to me, though hardly indicative of genius. Had he made preparation to pass the admission examinations? In wide-eyed wonder he confessed that he had never heard of such a thing; he had taken two years in the local high school, and had done fairly well. A college, he had thought, was open to everyone who wanted to learn, and he could scarcely conceive that anybody desired it more than he, or needed it more. Had he money? Only a few dollars; he had expected to pay his way by writing for magazines. What was one to do with such a lad? I should like to narrate that after the usual tribulations he succeeded, with such small aid as he could secure, in graduating brilliantly and afterwards became the great man whose name is on all your lips. The pathetic fact is that he plodded out into the fog again, headed for Ohio, and I have never seen him since, nor heard of him. It is true that he carried with him as much good counsel as a youth of six-and-twenty could give, and a vague promise or two from people of means who were reluctantly and semi-torpidly spending a part of the summer in town; and his lean pocket-book was not quite so hopelessly inadequate for the home journey.

There are many ways of getting into colleges. In the days of which I am speaking, one might at our institution score (in the years of one's lifetime) twenty-six "points" of admission credits, and then one was admitted; it was all done in examinations set by the college, but the candidate must also be recommended by his school and present a certificate of good moral character. At least, so it was "in principle," as the French say. In the college catalog were thirty pages of painfully fine print, telling exactly what subjects were to be taken, and exactly how much of each, and exactly how each was to be studied. To read those thirty pages was almost a liberal education in itself. In actual practice almost anybody was let in who had the price of his tuition (that was apparently the meaning of "good moral character") and could collect about half of the required "twenty-six points." The "points" which he failed to secure were counted against him as "conditions"—that is, additional infantile work to be performed during his college years. In other words, the more incompetent he had shown himself, the more he was expected to do. Now, that was one way of gaining admission to our college; but there was another. If a lad was unable to meet any of our scholastic demands, but had had some schooling and possessed the cash, he was taken in as a "special student," and might, if he had a brain and lived long enough, complete under our hospitable roof both his preparation for the collegiate course and his fruition of it. Had our unfortunate poet been able to exhibit a "good moral character," he might have gained entrance, despite his extreme youth, as a "special student." We sometimes think of showmen, patent medicine advocates, oil stock vendors, and Florida land speculators as liars; yet they are not far ahead of the college catalogs of the seventies and eighties and nineties. I suppose each college would have preferred to be truthful; but each felt itself obliged to outlie its competitors. It was like advertising; each fellow does it because the others do. Only quite recently have catalogs begun to approximate the truth in the statement of their requirements for admission; something of the time-honored tradition still lingers. It would indeed be odd if, in an age when food products and drugs are compelled to reveal their ingredients, and politicians their campaign expenses, the old habit of mendacity should be preserved in the academic world alone.

This business of sifting candidates is no easy matter. Methods are continually changing, and almost invariably for the better, but they are far from perfect; perhaps they always will be. The object is to take in as many of the desirable as possible, and to keep out as many as possible of the undesirable. How shall the college get my poet and exclude the son of my resourceful millionaire? I wish I knew the answer. The best of sifters will err in both directions.

On a large scale, the nation has the same problem as the college. I read last summer that the Portuguese government was making a strenuous effort to exclude undesirable elements from its territory. One cannot help asking one's self: who are the undesirables, in the eyes of the Portuguese? Are they the Argentines, the Armenians, and the Greeks? Shall the Armenian call the Argentine black? Or can it be that we ourselves are undesirables? The answer to that question depends on the answer to another: is there oil in Portugal? If so, we shall soon learn that American lives in that land need to be protected by our marines, and we may expect an outburst of patriotic fervor at home. American patriotic oratory, rotund though it be, has one defect—lack of spontaneity: it smells of the lamp, or, in other words, *sapit oleum*.

Amity consists, not in ignorance of other people's queerness, but in acceptance of it. "He iss a true frient, an' don't you forget it," declares Lew Field (in *Hanky Panky*, Act III, Scene 5). "Vot iss ut, a true frient?" inquires the innocent Weber. "A true frient iss a man dot knows shoost exactly vot you are and den forgets ut." An excellent definition.

A true friend, though, is also a poet. He may, in the back of his head, know what you really are; but he sees you always (or almost always) through a fog which hides all but your brightnesses. And he is willing any day, for your delectation, to let his own material world go up in smoke. Little Paul, in great excitement, telephoned to his wee comrade: "John, John, do you want to see a peach of a fire?" "Sure!" "Then come over to my house, as fast as you can. It's on fire. Hurry!"

As a parallel to the swiftness with which John responded, I can think only of the rapidity of a sea-gull answering with his presence the squawk of another gull which has found food. He arrives quicker, one would think, than sound can travel. And so do numberless companions. How they do come swarming up from nowhere, apparently condensing out of the air like snowflakes! But why does the first gull, the fortunate discoverer, give a call? Is it friendship; or is it an unconscious joyful reaction? One is inclined to take the latter explanation, when one watches the greedy squabble over tidbits. Seldom indeed have I seen an edible morsel remain in the possession of its first finder.

With an article not immediately edible the original owner may sometimes have better luck; for the grabbing habit seems to be impulsive rather than premeditated. A mussel or a snail or a crab or a sea-urchin has to be carried up in the air and broken open by dropping on a rock. Very often the possessor, immediately pursued, has to let his prey fall on a soft spot or from too little elevation. Thus one finds even grassy lawns on cliff-tops strewn with shells. Besides, I have my doubts whether an ordinary gull has sense enough, even if undisturbed, to carry out the process effectively. Gulls, presumably, are not much more intelligent than men; and the common run of men simply follow a routine. Having no comprehension of the principle of the thing, they usually omit the very details which make it effective. They put on their Sunday clothes and go to church, for instance, without ever a thought of opening their hearts to charity. Even so the conventional, unthinking gull starts skyward with its booty, but drops it in the mud. Occasionally, though, one observes a gull of superior mind, who, with manifest understanding of the game, plays it as it should be played. He will carry his snail over the ooze and the muck, over the pebbles and rubble, until he sees right under him a smooth rock; then he will fly straight upward ten feet or more, and at just the right moment you will see the black speck drop from his beak.

Perched on a spar-buoy like St. Simeon Stylites, a gull seems the type of solitude. Indeed, as a fisher he is an individualist, whether he watches from a rock or from the water's surface. But let abundance show itself, on sea or shore, he becomes gregarious. Is there any friendship in it, any sense of companionship? Every night, apparently, the whole community returns home to its breeding place on one of the Duck Islands—a land entirely theirs, protected by its potent smell; there I once helped out of its shell a baby gull that was clamoring to be born. In the daytime, too, when they rest, gulls like to sit together. One sees them in long shining rows on reefs and ridgepoles, all facing in the same direction. This beautiful concord, I judge, is due less to the beating of many hearts as one, than to a common disinclination to have their tail feathers ruffled, which makes them invariably roost with their faces to the wind. But which of us can afford to have his motives analyzed? A pretty spectacle of harmony our birds present, all resting in a white line, with faces to the fore, when the ridge of rock which supports them is beginning to recede into the foggy far-away.

DOES IT PAY TO ADVERTISE?

WE met at the village post office, where we had called for our daily bunch of contact with the busy world. He is a great manufacturer, producer of an article which you all certainly have long known by name, and probably all use every day. "And I am a doggerel bard"—or what you will—at any rate, a person of no importance. But we were alike in this, that ninety-five per cent. of our mail was made up of circulars, while four per cent. consisted of semicircular appeals for charity. Not on that day alone, nor in vacation time alone, but all through the year, with the exception of the flood seasons of the Christmas card and the Easter card—mountains of advertisement to anthills of news, just as in our dailies and weeklies, where it is a matter of acres to inches. If this be an exaggeration, I do not apologize: in your hearts you know a deliberate from an emotional misstatement; and a *crime passionnel* is sure to be forgiven. O genial and seductive Phineas T. Barnum, so venerated in our childhood, O that we should live to curse you!

"We producers and sellers," declared my manufacturing friend in answer to my inquiry whether all this solicitation was of any use to anybody, "we reckon that a three per cent. return is the highest we can ever expect from advertising. I advertise because the other fellow does, and he advertises because I do, and the profit of it goes neither to him nor to me, but to the publicity agent." "You have said it!" I cried, as one to whom the truth is revealed. "You have named the winner, the insatiable Moloch into whose mammoth maw our forests—or as much as the railroads and cigarettes have left of them—are vanishing, to be reborn as wastes of wearisome print which nobody ever reads, except (perhaps) the proof-reader. A bare, treeless, shadowless earth, one huge unmitigated spotlight, is the world our sons are to inherit!" I did not really cry all this, because my companion, having read his one postcard and dumped his armfull of advertisements into the waste-basket, had turned his face homeward; but I thought it.

I thought also, by way of compensation, that it could not last long, because the human race has evidently reached its last lap. Just consider the foregoing year, when, despite the unusually salubrious weather, everybody had a cold all winter long, and all through the spring, and on and on until summer rustication had partially cleansed his lungs of gasoline. For gasoline it is that is killing us—gasoline, next to advertising the greatest scourge of our day. Already mankind is divided into two classes, the gasoline-breathers and the air-breathers; and we are booked to witness a survival of the unfittest. Possibly, to be sure, we may develop gasoline-gills, and contrive to extricate sufficient oxygen from the medium that envelops us; but it is not likely—there is not time enough. In all probability the air-breathers will die out very shortly, and the earth will be left to the breathers of gasoline. Their triumph, however, will be brief. Not long after the death of their competitors, the world's supply of gasoline will be exhausted; and they, too, having nothing to breathe, will perish. Then old Dame Nature may begin afresh her discouraging experiment.

Meanwhile, the thought of extermination is made sweet by the pest of "publicity." That seems to be, nowadays, the barker's pet name for his latrating art. An art it is, beyond question—a highly developed, ingenious, interesting art, and extremely profitable to the barker, although I greatly doubt whether it benefits anyone else. Perhaps some people buy things because they have seen the names thereof again and again blazoned on bill-boards and blazing in electric constellations; but I fancy there are many who, like me, prefer an article whose cost has not been quadrupled by announcement. Really, I cannot recall ever in my life having been lured to a purchase by the Siren whistle of the advertiser; and I surely cannot be uniquely different. The example of the hen, in *It Pays to Advertise*, is more conducive to cachinnation than to conviction.

There is in latration, as in other arts, an infinite stretch of difference between the best and the ordinary—and none between the ordinary and the damnable.

Il n'y a point de degrés du médiocre au pire.

In a daily newssheet one begins a lurid, scare-headed yarn on the front page, but recoils from the effort to track it to the remote fastnesses whither it presently retreats, and the ambushed advertisements among which one was expected to stumble in its pursuit are left unseen. On the other hand, in a weekly story-paper, if one has the deftness and the desire to follow the flea-like jumps of an escaping narrative, the "publicity features" stirred to life by its saltatory progress are so manifestly its betters that the poor squirming tale finds itself forgotten. Still, entrancing as some of the present day achievements are, I believe the art has passed its meridian. Where now, on the pictorial side, is the equal of "Spotless Town," or, in the poetic field, the peer of the "Pantless Panthunter"?

No, the giants are dead. As in other realms of art, epigones succeed the masters, genius yields to stan-dardized mediocrity. Nearly all today's output smacks of the class-room; it leads the spectator to reflect: "If I had taken a course in the subject, I might have done that myself." A subway journey, once tingling with the possibility of delicious surprise, has become as humdrum as perusal of the admirable machine-made stories in a popular weekly. The exhibits now ranged before our defenseless eyes are interesting chiefly as examples of the psychological theories affected by the reigning school. Subways and trolley-cars are the best places to study them, inasmuch as these seats of compulsory concentration afford the advertiser his most favorable opportunity. If he cannot catch us there, he will probably never get us at all, although the cinematograph and the radio suggest possibliities as yet unfathomed. Theatre drop-curtains are good, too; but our country has not utilized them much, preferring to rely on the freely distributed program.

Program advertisements, while less intriguing than program music, furnish puzzles of their own, problems of selection and spacing, problems of appropriateness, of suiting the word to the mood. Yet I do not believe the publicity colleges devote a special course to them, for I have rarely seen a good one. In general they are simply transferred, with scant change or none, from a different atmosphere.

So it is, too, with the program jokes which, in corners unexpectedly left unsold, are shoved in to avert the ignominy of blankness. Hurriedly borrowed from Heaven knows there, these fortuitous *facetiae* are often surprisingly entertaining. But there lurks in them an element of mystery, often a poignant pathos, a note of helplessness, owing to their dependence on the number of lines in the vacant space they are to fill. Often, like the feet of Cinderella's wicked sisters, they are shorn of toes or heels to fit into the unyielding receptacle. One may find in a single pro-

gram a half dozen such mutilated waifs. Six Pleasan-
tries in Search of a Point, they come drifting out of
the nowhere into the here, only to drift back again,
unsatisfied. "'My watch is a runabout,'" you read.
"'What kind of watch is a runabout?'" And that is the
end—but no, by good luck, you discover, in isolated
irrelevance eight pages further on: "'It runs about
two minutes and then stops.'"—"'I got this bracelet
from a millionaire,' said Mayme to Edythe. 'What's
his name?' Edythe inquired." And his name would
forever elude you, did there not magically emerge
from the depths of your memory: "'Woolworth.'"—
"'Can't you help an old lady to alight?' asked a
chauffeur of a young bystander. 'Sure!' was the
answer." Of course, the story is well rounded and edi-
fyingly ended, yet there rankles in you a sense of in-
completeness until, a few years later, you find version
O in another program: "'Can't you help an old lady
to a light?' 'Sure! where's her cigarette?'"—Or, it
may be not the conclusion but the beginning that has
been pruned away. "'Scotch?' slyly inquired the
inspector. 'No,' said the expressman, 'Airedale.'"
Never will it cease to haunt me.—Sometimes, but
rarely, the middle has been excised. Here is an example of such evisceration: "'What is your name?'
asked Mrs. Newrich of the chauffeur her husband had
just engaged. 'My whole name, ma'am, is James
Darling.' 'Very well, James, you may drive on.'"
Can you reconstruct the story? I think I can. It

probably ran like this: " 'What is your name?' asked Mrs. Newrich of the chauffeur her husband had just engaged. 'James, ma'am.' 'My good man, we never call our chauffeurs by their first names. What is your whole name?' 'My whole name, ma'am, is James Darling.' 'Very well, James, you may drive on.' "

Here is a good field for students interested in the literary transmission of tales; but I must not explore it further, lest I lose my thread.

The proper study of a publicity agent, or of a publication agent, is the public. "Give the public what it wants," is the editor's motto. "Make the public want what you have to sell," is the device of the advertiser. And both mean the same. Here are two events that were featured a couple of summers ago in the same issue of an excellent journal: "One Hundred Injured as Crowd of 60,000 Riots to View the Bier of Valentino"; "Woman Wins at Clam Eating" ("continued on page nine, column 6"), with a picture of the fair "Champion Clam Eater Beginning Third Peck." Now the editor had evidently expected to make his principal item the funeral of President Eliot, which occurred at the same time; but the aforementioned world-shaking events threw it into the shade. Renan used to think that Shakespere's Caliban represented the Public; a better representative, it often seems to me, was Fred Stone's Scarecrow, in *The Wizard of Oz*, who had a lot of junk in his head instead of brains. But perhaps the Public, after all, is not quite such a fool as the advertiser wants it to be and the newspaper makes it out. Both, at any rate, do their best to increase its foolishness.

Our American public is, above all things, ingenuous. It is ingenuous because it has no standards; and it has no standards because, never having read anything worth reading, it cannot profit by others' experience, past or present. Hence it is easily buncoed by the first humbug that calls itself "new"—"the new religion," "the new art," "the new poetry," "the new education," or what not. There is a versifier whom I shall call Grosvenor, the very personification of prosy platitude. Correct and simple in his technique, he says the things which "all have thought," and which all who have written at all have expressed better. His commonplaceness is exceeded only by his popularity. A constant market awaits his wares; he is in brisk demand—at a dizzy price—to read his products before women's clubs throughout our land. Then there is Bunthorne, whom nobody understands—who, having in his vacuity no bottom, is unfathomable—who is so cunningly and unremittingly unrhythmical that he cannot be read aloud, even by the loosest-jawed. He, too, is a pet, like Klopstock more praised than perused, to be sure, but revered by the ladies and by the high-brow critics. How have both these types succeeded in imposing themselves? Both owe their fame, I believe, to the firm national conviction that poetry is by its very essence incomprehensible. Bunthorne, supremely incomprehensible because there is in him nothing to comprehend, is in our eyes the typical poet, awesomely unapproachable. Expecting to grasp nothing, far from being disappointed we are comfortably reassured; and we are respectfully thankful to the great man for running true to type, keeping the traditional distance, even with some extension. Grosvenor, on the other hand, is a delightful surprise; contrary to all experience, we find ourselves actually understanding him, actually understanding words that have been woven into verse; and our self-esteem naturally shoots up a hundred points. Grateful indeed we must be to the artist who can at the same time be a poet and be understood. Whether his poetry is good poetry is a question that never arises. As Dr. Johnson said of the dog who had been taught to walk on his hind legs: "It is not done well; but you are surprised to find it done at all."

By way of contrast, I met a real poet not long ago. It was only for a minute or two; but I had read some of his work, and I shall not forget his face. It was exactly what a young poet's face should be—frank, manly, sincere, sensitive, delicate, beautiful, like his verse. He was just eighteen, but already "old as the world," like Marchbanks. Only a handful of the oldest and best could qualify as peers of this modest and unknown boy. Think of it! Youthful poetry that is neither affected nor eccentric, neither vapid nor obscure; a young poet whose endeavor is not to be different but to be good among the good. I have high hopes of him; and so, rather shyly, has his father.

I wonder whether, in general, it is an advantage to an author to be personally known. Despite the evidence of this particular case, I suspect it is not usually profitable. Very seldom, I fancy, does the face fit the work; seldom is the man compatible with the creative mind that inhabits him. Few things let me down more than introduction to a great writer, a great painter, a great actor. It really is not fair. And it is not fair to the artist, in a biography of him or even in our own opinion, to average his home personality with his inspired self. An artist should be judged by his art. And for most artists the counsel of prudence is to hide behind it, remembering what familiarity breeds. One successful author of fiction has been off and on my friend from early years, and in boyhood we were closely associated. The result is that while I enjoy his work, I cannot admire it as strangers do: I am continually translating his mature effusions into terms of his puerile fancy; I hear in every sentence his adolescent voice; every sentiment awakens reminiscence of his erstwhile sentimentality, once appropriately mawkish. "Just like dear old Ned!" I say, and smile.

Recognition is a curious phenomenon. Have you ever asked yourself what it is that constitutes evidence of identity? How do you know the voice of an

acquaintance over the telephone? It is marvelous
enough that the diabolical instrument should transmit words at all; but to transmit them with the
precise timbre of the voice, so that the hearer can
immediately tell who is speaking—how can it? In
general, I suppose, we think we identify people by
their faces, when we see them on the street. I doubt it.
You will doubt it, too, if at any time you have
suffered from partial loss of sight. The face is not
the greatest tell-tale. Shape, gait, pose, these are the
prime characteristics. Much depends, too, on the
setting. Yesterday I saw across the way a young man
with whom I exchanged a friendly bow and smile;
and ever since that moment I have fruitlessly racked
my brain to remember who he is. He is someone I
know rather intimately. I can hear his voice, with its
customary intonations. I can picture the peculiar
poises of his head. I can recall my own somewhat
conflicting reactions to his personality. But who he is,
I cannot, cannot guess. The spot where he appeared
to me was not his usual spot.

I fancy an advertisement, in the highest reaches of
the art, awakens a train of reminiscence and at the
same time confounds you with strangeness. It must be
both conventional and jolting. "Pies like mother used
to make" carries you sweetly back into a past where
every viand was toothsome. But the ensuing variant
takes one step further, wedding tender memory to
startled expectation. "Impressions like mother used
to make" correlates the behind and the before.

A special branch of advertising is the annual or less-than-annual appeal of charitable organizations. I estimate that the typical man receives on the average at least two a day, all representing good causes and urgent needs. The multiplicity of social assistance in our country is beautiful to contemplate. But what is the puzzled typical man to do? To contribute, never so modestly, to all the deserving societies and institutes would consume more than his entire income, and it breaks his heart to refuse any. He must choose; on what basis shall the choice be made? How would it do to pick out not the "undeserving poor," but the enterprises which issue the poorest circulars? They presumably devote less money to overhead expenses, having no publicity man to pay, or at best a very cheap one; and, on the other hand, being inexpert in solicitation, they surely need your dollar worse than do those organizations whose "open sesame" is more imperiously addressed to your pocket-book. Prefer the frank, unblushing, printed, one-cent circular to the two-cented fake personal letter. Learn to look with cynical suspicion on expensive photogravures of incredibly emaciated children or incredibly intellectual colored students. Calculate the frequency with which libraries are burned down and dormitories need enlargement. Consider whether you can reconcile with your democratic principles a moneyed hierarchy such as this: Founder ($1000), Benefactor ($500), Donor ($250), Patron ($125), Fellow ($62.50), Charter Member ($31.25), Sustaining Member

:

($15.63), Annual Member ($7.82), Contributing
Member ($3.91), and Member—just plain "eggs"
($2.00). Note how your impulsive and supposedly
isolated "gift" of yesteryear has become your "annual subscription" for the current twelvemonth.
Observe how the wily philanthropist creeps up on
you, accelerating your periodicity by sending his
notice a fortnight earlier year by year. I do not
criticize these methods, all adopted for a worthy end;
I merely suggest that bodies which reap the advantage of them probably need your obol less than do the
unimaginative committees to which such artistry
has never occurred.

The right ratio and the correct kind of advertising:
that is a problem which nowadays confronts even
the churches, hitherto serenely supermundane. You
may turn them into charity bureaus or into community centers, with dances, radio, movies, and
bridge parties; that may prolong considerably their
corporate existence, but does it conserve their religious efficiency? Really it is a confession that religion
will no longer sell without megaphoning. What is the
matter with our churches? To an outsider the trouble
seems to be that there is not enough hell in them.
They appear to thrive exactly in proportion to the
heat of their hell. The pleasures of paradise are to
some extent a drawing card, but in Christian churches
they are over tenuous. I am told that the most fiercely
religious people in the world are the Muslim, whose

heaven is described as a sublimated red light district. We occidentals have to rely on hell and our hell is cooling. As paradise pales and as hell-fire fades, churches seem to decline. We have probably made a mistake in trying to turn religion into a thing of the intellect. Religion is essentially emotional. Philosophy is of the mind, religion of the heart—to use an old-fashioned terminology. The heart frequently prompts to right doing, but seldom to clear thinking. Can we get a modicum both of right doing and of clear thinking from philosophy alone? If so, the function of the ecclesiastical establishment becomes problematical. As its teaching grows more and more rationalistic, the more insistent looms the question: *Cui bono?* If St. Paul should now visit the Athens of America, he would doubtless opine that we are not superstitious enough. After all, can it be that superstition is, if not the principal ingredient, at least an essential element in religion? It certainly plays a leading rôle in politics, and has a speaking part in science. In a psychic activity which is primarily of the emotions, ought not superstition to be more prominent than in science, which is supposed to be purely intellectual, or in politics, wherein the lay intellect is presumed to have a considerable share?

What is a superstition? It is a belief which has been discarded, or never accepted, by the person who calls it by that name. To the believer, of course, it is not a superstition, but a fact. The dividing line is nebulous,

and shifts with the point of view. Not only are the
superstitions of today the beliefs of yesterday: it
sometimes happens that yesterday's superstitions are
today's beliefs. And contemporaneously, the tenets of
one nation are its neighbor's jests. "Vérité au deça
des Pyrénées, erreur au delà." For instance, when I
was a student in Germany I was solemnly warned,
again and again, that sleeping with my windows open
would make me blind. This credence, widely diffused
in Europe, perhaps owes its rise to some magic of
forgotten times. Whatever its origin, it is still an
article of faith even among the enlightened. During
a winter which my family and I spent at Cannes
there came to our hotel a Parisian lady whose lungs
were delicate. Promptly she began to grow stronger,
and with strength came recklessness. Having observed that we kept our windows open at night, she
wrote to her doctor in Paris asking whether she
might venture to open hers an inch or so, in view of
the mildness of the climate. "No," he replied, "while
it would be safe enough as far as your lungs are con-
cerned, it would be extremely dangerous for your
eyes." Another atmospheric fancy prevails among the
French. The bravest people in the world, they are
mortally afraid of a draft. The faintest puff of a
courant d'air excites them as a mouse upsets an ele-
phant. To sit between two windows is more deadly
than standing under a tree in a thunder-storm. However, they are themselves not wholly unconscious of

the humor of this phobia. A cartoon in one of their comic papers represents a gentleman transfixed by a huge knife in the hand of an Apache. "Don't pull it out," entreats the victim, "you'll make a draft!" Firmly rooted in our own soil, on the other hand, was (and probably is) the very ancient conviction that the moon shining on one's face during slumber will drive one insane. How prevalent this notion is nowadays in other countries, I cannot tell. For years it kept me in an agony of apprehension. According to a milder version of the tale, moonshine provokes not madness but somnambulism; and, for aught I know, this may be true.

To attain maximum results, I fancy the ecclesiastical barker ought to sell superstition, instead of philosophy, psychology, ethics, sociology, and politics; although all these lines of goods have been successfully sold by efficient salesmen. After all, the personality of the salesman is what counts most, whatever be his line. Into a village of self-respecting Yankees, mostly skippers, who punctiliously refer to one another as "Mr.," sails a big blond promotor, and approaching a group of notables engaged in earnest conversation, gives one of them, whom he has met two or three times before, a resounding thump on the back, hands him a punk cigar and shouts: "Well, Si, old man, how goes it? Put this in your pocket and smoke it for my sake." You may be pretty sure he has wasted his cabbage; and if the loss be small, it is all the more certain. I am not surprised that drummers from the United States have been slow to make their way in Latin countries.

Once, at the Odéon, I saw Molière's M. Jourdain acted in an unusual way—as a new-rich person who is ridiculous merely from ignorance. Far from the irresistibly amusing blockhead that Thiron used to make him at the Comédie Française, he was a man of sprightly intelligence, always wide-awake, and impatient to learn. Unhappily there were so many things to learn that there seemed to be no place to begin, and he never got started. Thiron's impersonation, I am sure, was closer to the Master's conception; but this fresh interpretation was legitimate and highly entertaining. And it reminded me strangely of so many people at home!

Consider what, in a people of the renovated Jourdain type, would be the dominant superstitions. I fancy they would be three: first, faith in the innate goodness of man (one's self being the typical man); second, belief that the newest is always the best; third (and the third is the greatest of these), the conviction that it always pays to advertise.

PROPAGANDA

ONE special type of advertising is propaganda. It differs from the ordinary kind in that it is not carried on primarily for money, but it seems to be subject to the same general laws and to the same query concerning its profitableness.

On this question one procures the greatest abundance of evidence during an international conflict. Let us suppose that one party, a devotee of preparedness, has its advertising matter all ready. Paflagonia, let us say, has a tremendous start; and all through the first year only Paflagonian pamphlets flood the world. One simple (but traveled) neutral citizen gets at least a good ton of them. What is the result? As long as the condition lasts, throughout the whole Paflagonia-inundated territory, nobody doubts for a moment that Paflagonia, with a wretched cat's-paw or two, is alone to blame for the catastrophe. Fiendishly she has been contriving the whole infernal business for years and years; at a long-awaited and carefully selected moment she has fired the mine. Every Paflagonian pamphlet confirms this opinion; the louder Paflagonia protests, the shriller Paflagonia shrieks, the firmer this belief becomes. Every utterance, every silence (if there be any) is a corroboration.

Not until the second year, let us say, does the party of the second part find an articulate voice· Then the tide turns, and we are submerged under the eloquence of Crimtartary. At this point a few doubting Thomases venture to suggest that after all there may be something on the other side. As the tide rises the whisper becomes a plea, and Crimtartary comes in for her share of the responsibility— a share that grows with the opening of Crimtartary's floodgates.

An observer in far-off Atlantis cannot fail to be interested in this battle of the books, especially if he knows both the principal contestants pretty well, and can interpret their appeals in terms of their complexes. Of course he cannot read everything in that first year, ash-can after ash-can goes forth from his cellar stuffed with propagandist eloquence. If he has been a student abroad, he gets more than his share of the deluge. But his reaction is identical with that of his less bombarded neighbor. Every plea operates as a confession—a peculiarly shocking confession, too. Why is it? *Qui s'excuse s'accuse*, of course. But there seems to be something at work more potent than natural distrust of the lady who protests too much. The propaganda, somehow, is all wrong. The wrongness, indeed, is not confined to the Paflagonian output; but inasmuch as Paflagonia has spoken first and

loudest, her cataract of words impresses the far-off
observer as a more toadlike and snakelike spewing
than the spirts from Crimtartary's mouth. By the
time the latter nation and her friends turn on their
grandes eaux, the far-off observer has become a bit
hardened to the recital of the thing which is not;
besides, he is tired, he has made up his mind, and he
does not read so diligently.

The example of all this worse than wasted power
may suggest to us some of the things which propagandist advertising should not be. Like other publicity, it should not be obviously mendacious. More or
less mendacious, of course, it must be—that is the
essence of advertising; but its mendacity must not be
obvious to babes and fools. When, for instance, a
group of eminent men unites in denying something
which the whole world knows to be true, only loss can
result. No, in propaganda, as in other publicity, one
must lie with some adroitness. In this respect the
second advertiser in the field has a chance to profit by
the lesson of the first.

Closely akin to this first maxim is a principle which
really includes it: the propagandist must not reveal
too manifestly his contempt for the intelligence of his
public. Now, although the reader of advertisements
presumably is a fool, he does not like to be told so,
unless very covertly. An unmistakable assumption of
his idiocy is liable to prejudice him against the advertiser. And most of the matter let loose on us in a

hectic war-year is evidently based on that warrantable but unwise assumption.

Nearly as disastrous is the assumption of moral, social, or mental superiority on the part of the propagandist. The dwellers in Atlantis are not (and can you blame them?) allured by the conception of a Zenda divinely chosen to conquer and civilize the rest of the world; and that idea—doubtless quite unbeknown to the writers, so axiomatic has it become to them—forms the major premise of most of the Zendist syllogisms. I do not say that it is wrong for a nation to regard itself as the chosen people; probably all nations cherish such an illusion. I say merely that from the advertiser's point of view it is unwise to allow that notion to dominate one's "publicity."

If it requires a great war to teach the peace-time propagandist how to avoid pitfalls, I cannot say the result justifies the expense. Commercial advertising, to be sure, generally dodges them; but the disinterested mission, with its eyes bent on the stars, drops in as easily as the astronomer into the well. It regularly assumes moral superiority for itself, superior asininity for its listener, and a superlatively mendacious tone toward the vice it wishes to correct, believing that to lie about sin is not sinful. I know all these things, having done them all myself, on behalf of sundry good causes. These mistakes do not exhaust our list; we are very fertile. Probably our commonest military error consists in training our artillery on an open door. *Enfoncer une porte ouverte*—that seems to be the action that consumes most of our ammunition. Instead of overcoming the real obstacles to our cause, we keep hammering away at imaginary works or at defences long since abandoned. This, too, I have done (and shall doubtless do again). The very hardest thing in our campaign is to place our shot where it will do the most good, or—abandoning the warlike figure which is becoming rather intricate for a civilian—to make the heathen read our tracts. A tract is commonly written by a missionary for other missionaries, who read it with great lip-smacking. It is perused also, with more or less satisfaction, by contributors to the cause. And the Board wonders how the heathen can resist it. Yet the answer is easy. The heathen resist because not one of them ever reads the irresistible appeal. Some instinct saves them. "Ain't them heathen converted yet?" cried the indignant captain of industry when approached by a collector for the missions. "Why, I gave fifty cents to convert 'em a year ago!"

To cure the sick man, you must make him take your remedy (you see I am changing my figure again, like a lady who follows the fashions). And he will not take your dose if he knows what it is. He has heard often enough the old arguments by which the forsaken defences have again and again been battered down. His mind is made up; he knows the pros and cons, and is not going to waste any time on it; the.

business does not interest him, anyhow. The docile
convert, to be sure, will lap up all the sop you offer
him; but what is the use? Why preach to those who
already believe—who, possibly, are stauncher be-
lievers than you are? For it is very hard to keep un-
shaken faith in a doctrine you have been preaching
a long time, especially if, like me, you are an over
modest man. How is the word of life to be got into
those other people—those who live a living death?
Forcible feeding is out of the question. There is only
one way—deceit, a flank movement, a sugar-coated
pill.

The commercial folk discovered this long ago.
Witness the reading advertisement, the purposeful
"story," the teleological photogravure sheet. The two
greatest experts at this sort of propaganda are Morris
Gest and Tut-Ank-Amen. Just remember the newspaper pages they filled, day after day, week after
week, month after month, the one with his *Miracle*,
the other with his unhappily violated tomb. Tut-Ank,
being the elder, was the more successful; he carried
on longer, and during a great part of the time he
secured space on the front page. To my mind, they
both overdid it; but perhaps I am more sensitive than
the majority Certainly hosts of readers fell, and fell
hard. As for me, I did go to see *The Miracle*; I went,
though, already prepared to be disappointed, and I
was. To the Tut-Ank deluge I was more than ready to
say Amen forty days and forty nights before it began

to subside. Indeed, I was so utterly fed up, cloyed,
stuffed, hypertrophied, and nauseated that I refused
to visit his old tomb when I was in Egypt, whereas I
did look in at the graves of several worthies who had
maintained a dignified silence. In spite of everything,
though, I had to see all of Tut-Ank's real Louis XV
furniture in the Museum of Cairo.

A great publisher, himself a successful author, and
one of the Old Guard of Spelling Reform, asked me
to write a little puff of that movement for a new
magazine he was starting. In the resulting article I
followed the indirect method I have just advocated.
I began with a poetic description of the sky-line of
New York City and gradually—very gradually—slid
off into the contours of English printed words. Just as
in Conrad's *Lord Jim*, the reader would have had no
idea what it was all about until he was two-thirds
through; and then (as I calculated) it would have
been too late for him to extricate himself from the
quicksand. I put these verbs into the conditional
because the experiment never came off. My dear old
friend, the editor, felt his feet grow frigid; he was
afraid, he confessed, that his subscribers would be
puzzled to the irritation point if they accidentally
started on a screed of which they could not foresee the
end. Readers, he said, do not like surprises. Therefore
he begged me to let him substitute a fresh exordium
of his own composition, conceived in the time-
honored vein. Of course I had to consent, and our

joint product appeared, as plainly jointed as Barnum's mermaid or the half-female bull of Taormina.
According to careful statistics, it was read by four
persons: the editor, the printer, the proof-reader, and
me.

Conventionally, one should begin a spelling-reform
plea with a table, showing the preposterous number
of spellings which English usage makes possible for a
single sound, and the preposterous number of sounds
that may be indicated by a single spelling. There is no
end to this material, and the exhibition of it can be
made very amusing. To be sure, most literate people
are more or less familiar with it already; but there
are always some greenhorns who at such a display
open wide their innocent eyes and mouths. Even
to the sophisticated, there is something incredibly
monstrous in the picture; to match its enormity one
must turn to the distances of the stars or the ages of
the nebulae. Indeed, it is so funny that some think it
would be a pity to spoil the joke.

After that, one passes to the historical side and
shows how many of our supposedly instructive spellings are due to etymological blunders, to the Dutchi-
ness of foreign printers, to love of ornamental
flourish. Here one may pause to point out how in-
finitesimally small is the number of those users of
English who could derive any profit from the etymological hints conveyed by our spellings, even if these
were all correct. One may add that only words of

philological interest to any but professed linguists are those of Latin origin, and that these would be little affected by any reform measure likely to be adopted. Here is a natural place for the statement that a change of orthography does not obliterate the evidence of the ages, inasmuch as nobody has proposed the destruction of the written and printed matter now in existence.

The next theme is the time-saving argument. As compared with the Italian or Spanish child, whose educational outfit includes no spelling-book, the English pupil wastes on the acquisition of his strangely composite orthography a period estimated by ultra-conservatives as a twelvemonth, by radicals as two or three years. During this year or these years, it is urged, the schoolboy might be getting information that is intrinsically valuable. But the waste by no means ends there. All through life, whenever we write, or print, or read, we devote a considerable share of our effort to the fabrication or recognition of characters which in a phonetic system would disappear. The late Henry Holt, one of our foremost publishers, ingeniously calculated the loss, in dollars, caused every year, in the United States, by printing useless letters. It mounts into the millions, if you count printers' time, cost of paper, and all the other items. He reckoned it up in a curious pamphlet, wherein he estimated also the amount of good things, the stores of comfort and happiness, which these millions would buy. On such thoughts he loved to dwell. "How much does love in a cottage cost?" he once asked of Andrew Carnegie, who was presiding at a great Simplified Spelling banquet in the Waldorf Astoria. "I don't know," promptly cried the genial iron-master, "but whatever it costs, it is worth it." Possibly it is worth the sacrifice of a silent letter or two.

A stronger plea than that, inasmuch as it apeals straight to our great national softness for children, is the following: because our orthography, being quite unsystematic, must be learned outright like the multiplication table, every attempt to use rational methods being fatal, and because a very large part of the pupil's time and energy at a most sensitive age has to be devoted to this study in which logic has no part, all the earlier schooling of our children is a process of stultification, from which most of them never recover. It breeds that distrust of reason which seems to be characteristic of the English-speaking nations. And it constitutes a cruel inhibition of the childish mental activity, which is naturally logical.

You see how the propagandist moves on, first showing you how ridiculous you are, then how prodigal you are, and lastly how wicked you are. See here! Will you accept my doctrine, or will you stand convicted of ridiculousness, prodigality, and wickedness? Now, people do not like to be thus forcibly convinced. When such argumentation is backed by rope

or faggot, to be sure, it generally converts. But when
there is behind it no secular arm, it usually fails to pin
the pagan.

The absurdity of current usage the pagan readily
admits; it is one of the many absurdities of custom
and of nature. What is more absurd than the weather?
Yet we put up with it. If he remembers that other
peoples have in considerable measure rid themselves
of the orthographic encumbrance, he reflects also
that other peoples are different and our conduct is
not to be governed by theirs. As to the extravagance
of our present course, that does stagger him for a
moment, then he begins to guess that the expense has
been "grossly exaggerated." Anyhow, he contends,
we have to compare the cost of maintenance with the
cost and the trouble of change; and while the maintenance charge is spread over many generations, the
bother and expense of shifting fall upon his particular
generation alone. That settles it. The moral appeal he
does not understand very well, not being versed in
psychology. When he was a boy, they had to learn
things by heart, and it will do the present boys and
girls no harm to have their noses held to the grind-
stone. Things are made too easy for them, altogether.
There seems to be no proof of the statement that it
injures their brains to learn to spell. They do not
learn it well enough to hurt them much.

Thus do the heathen react to the gospel, when it
reaches them at all. Now and then, however, appears

a potential convert, an unbeliever with the will to believe, if he only knew what to believe in. For there is perplexing disagreement among the apostles. Their gift of tongues smacks less of Pentecost than of Babel. At least, it used to be so. The younger reformers are drawing together in large groups, and there will doubtless be an approach to harmony when the elder statesmen are all gone. The reformers of the newer type are not so desperately in earnest, having lost some of their faith in hell; and they are willing to admit the possibility of quasi-salvation through a church other than their own. It must be admitted that while they have notably increased the chance of success, they are not nearly so picturesque as the die-hard individualists, each of them wedded to his special system—the only way, the only truth, the only life; each a Simeon Stylites, solitary on his isolated column. Now that reformers have climbed down from their eminence, they can get together. But there were some grand old giants among the Simeons.

Half a dozen years ago I received a long letter from an English gentleman, quite unknown to me, whom I shall call Epaminondas Dixon. His name is really quite as original as that—indeed, a bit more so. He had somehow got hold of my address in connection with spelling reform, and that being the ruling passion of his life, he had to make contact with me. I do not yet know, after some six years' correspondence,

what his business is, what his career, nor whence his
extraordinary name. I know that he is something of
an artist, that he makes beautiful picture post-cards,
that he lives in a retired and attractive spot in England, that he has been in America (even in Boston,
my native town), and that he remembers everything
he has ever seen. I know that he is an elderly man; in
a recent letter he announced that he expected to live
but two years longer. I know that he ardently loves
his mother tongue, whose purity he would preserve
by excluding all loans, neologisms, and periphrases.
I know that he has his own system of phonetic spelling
which, in his second letter, he begged me to criticize. Happily I was able to say with truth that it was
as good a broad one-language system as I had ever
seen. I even wrote him, to his intense delight, an
epistle of some length in his own notation. I felt
obliged to add that it seemed to me futile for each
phonetician to cling to his own method, however
good it might be, the one chance of victory lying in a
united front. He agreed about the united front, but
declared the front must unite under his banner.

One more thing I know about Mr. Dixon. I know
that he is economical of paper. And inasmuch as he is
rather a voluminous correspondent, he uses for a
letter a number of scraps of different sizes, and writes
all over them. His hand, however, is neat and clear;
his style, forceful, terse, correct. Furthermore (this I
discovered only two years ago) he has the habit of

bringing his casually acquired acquaintances into communication with one another, thus creating, as it were, a constellation of variegated eccentrics, known to one another through him, who is but dimly known to any. The method he follows is to send a letter from a correspondent in Java to one in Iceland who may be interested, with a request that both the letter and the answer to it be eventually forwarded to him.

For instance, I happened to remark in the course of a communication to Mr. Dixon that the only European spelling worse than the English, as far as I knew, was the Irish. Some months later I received a message from an Irishman, resident in Alaska, to whom my epistle had been sent. Luckily he is a very gentle Irishman, a scholar, an enthusiastic nationalist, a fanatical admirer of his native language and literature, which he regards as the world's choicest. He, too, is rather an aged man according to his estimate. He writes freely, with an old-fashioned, Addisonian eloquence and an uncommonly rich vocabulary. Evidently he has long been in Alaska. Why, I cannot guess. Several times have I heard from him. His latest missive contained a full description of Irish spelling and pronunciation, with a well developed outline of Irish grammar, all written in his copperplate hand. Having observed, he said, that I was interested in his language, he had taken pleasure in occupying the intervals in his business, for many months, in the composition of this work for me.

As far as I am competent to judge, it is a really valuable contribution to the study of modern Irish. I certainly have studied it with great interest. Among other things, I have learned to pronounce his name, and thereby have got a more favorable opinion of its orthography.

Irish spelling is an awful thing, if the words be spoken as the English speak them. Uttered in the Irish fashion, they fit well enough their bewildering notation. It seems the Hibernian system of writing is perfectly regular, if one but follow strictly a very complicated set of rules. I am told that something of the sort is true of Russian. Reformers have tried to apply this idea to English, but without much success: in the chaos of English usage there is scarcely any material for a logical structure. The nearest approach to such a method is found in the plan of the British Simplified Spelling Society, of which Professor Gilbert Murray is President. On the other hand, the American Simplified Spelling Board, rejecting for the present the idea of a thorough-going logic, has pursued consistently the course hitherto followed in a blindly casual way by the English language, treating piecemeal those words, or classes of words, whose apparent abnormalities can be cured without introducing new trouble. Though greatly interested in both these experiments, and willing to assist in both, I cannot believe that either will go very far. The British campaign will bring about a respelling of the whole vocabulary by a very few people, the American will result in the respelling of a few words by a great many people; and both, I hope, will prepare the way for a general revision on a phonetic basis, which alone, hard though it appear to introduce, may ultimately give satisfaction. This, of course, is one of the aims of the International Phonetic Association.

I do believe, after all, that a real cure will be no more difficult to administer than a palliative, if it be administered at the right time: namely, at the moment of shift from one generation to another. That is, let the children learn to read first with a phonetic alphabet, and let that alphabet be used subsequently in all statements of pronunciation; and the worst is done. You have a generation at home in the new spelling and the old, ready to encourage its successor to discard the old style altogether, except for antiquarian purposes. As to the process of teaching the little ones to read by means of phonetic texts, and then changing to the standard orthography, there has been enough actual experience to show that it effects rather a gain than a loss in time; according to all testimony, the transition is astonishingly easy. Thus can be met in some measure the objection that a change puts all the cost on one generation. The reason why most people are reluctant to consent to orthographic innovation is that they have a capital invested in the old style: having devoted a great deal of time and trouble to the acquisition of it, they do not want to throw it away. The proposed course of procedure would not compel them to do so.

A strange thing, to be sure, always looks ludicrous. During the visit of the French war-time delegation headed by Joffre and Viviani, as I stood in the crowd watching the arrival of the distinguished group, I was accosted by a fellow-citizen at my side, who, removing his clay pipe from his mouth, delivered himself as follows: "Thim fellers from acrass the watter is funnylookun fellers." "Perhaps," I retorted, "we look as funny to them as they look to us." This he considered for a moment; then solemnly declared: "They ain't anny of us looks as funny as thim fellers from acrass the watter." When all is said and done, the chief obstacle to a new spelling is that it "looks funny." Regarded, however, in the first place, not as a substitute but as an auxiliary, it loses much of its funniness. Nobody sees anything particularly amusing in the extraordinary combinations of letters sometimes used by dictionaries to mark pronunciation.

Familiar things not only look to us fitting; they even look beautiful, when there is a question of exchanging them for something unfamiliar. The poet Rostand once wrote that to spell the word *cygne* with an *i* would be robbing the swan of its reflection in the water. A pretty conceit. Some people take an aesthetic satisfaction in the rugged outlines of our English orthography. This is a matter of taste, about which there must be no disputing. To Andrew Carnegie the *gh*'s, which to others are suggestive of Alpine sublimity, were an eyesore. I have heard him say that he would gladly sacrifice a considerable part of his considerable fortune "to get all the *gh*'s out of the spelling-book." This is odd for a Scotchman whose grandfather actually pronounced the *gh* in *thorough*. To whichever opinion each one of us may incline, we must all agree that the opinion, whatever it is, begins and ends with the individual. It is not hereditary. It is not absolute. A *gh* is lovely or odious, not in itself, but according to each individual's way of looking at it. And a generation brought up in a *gh*-less sunshine will never miss the *gh*'s gentle shade.

For myself, I can say that I sympathize with both parties. Naturally fond of what is old, I cannot quite repress a sneaking partiality for the rotten old spelling, which glowered upon my impressionable childhood. Yet the moment reason comes into play, the moment the critical faculty awakes, I can see that the ancient makeshift is as ugly as sin—I might say, uglier. It violates the fundamental principle of my aesthetics, namely, that a thing should be adapted to its use. If the use of spelling is to suggest concepts, the Chinese ideographs would seem to suit the purpose far better, even though they have lost their obviously pictorial character. If, on the other hand, its function is to represent the sounds of speech, nothing else used

by civilization is quite so inadequate—not even tongs,
shutter-fasteners, cream-pitchers, English weights
and measures, or pounds, shillings, and pence. Every
time I spell a word (with my critical faculty awake) I
feel as a man ploughing with a log of wood or trying
to shave with a stone razor. Peculiarly outraged is my
sense of fitness if I happen to spell the word correctly;
for the conventionally "correct" spelling is generally
the one most at odds with logic. And logic is sym-
metry, which is beauty. No, when you come to think
of it, nothing can be uglier than our so-called orthography, considered as an interpreter of the words we
speak.

"But," you will say, if you are a really thoughtful
objector, and not a merely impressionistic one, "spelling is no longer a representation of sounds. It has its
own separate existence, like a shadow which shall
have detached itself and walked away. Letters no
longer suggest sounds. We have become a race of eye-
readers; in fact, silent reading is now a ruling fad in
our schools. We have, indeed, two languages: a
printed one, which is communicated, with no auditory sense, from page to eye; and a spoken one, communicated by mouth to ear. And these two have no
contact save in the thought which both express, just
as spirit and matter are cognizant of each other only
in God. Of course it is a burden to have two languages to learn as one's mother tongue—to have, as
it were, one's mother tongue split like a viper's; but

the mischief is done and there is no undoing it. Besides, we have in compensation an immense gain in rapidity when it comes to reading. Let us read, read, read, and forget how to talk. Then our linguistic outfit will be reduced again to one medium. Poetry, alas! must go by the board, and even prose style, for they require the auditory impression in both writer and reader. In fact, there will soon be no aesthetic appreciation whatever in the act of reading; we shall read only for the sense, and we shall get it fast—so fast that a Sunday paper will not last through a breakfast, nor a Congressional report through a subway ride. Waste no more time in talking or in listening, but read!" Thus, O thoughtful objector, do you thoughtfully object to all the arguments that have preceded. Nor will I answer you. Thoughtful objectors are so few that their vote may be disregarded.

Indeed, now that I think of it, there is really no need of answering anybody except printers and typists, for in another generation they will be the only people who shall not have forgotten how to spell.

DOGS

WERE you ever told that dogs bite only naughty boys? Don't you believe it. Dogs are like the wind: they bite where they list. And, like the wind, they are variable. For reliability give me a cat. I once had a cat named Moses, who used to come to meet me every day as I returned home. While I was absent for a week, he would wander disconsolately around my study, meowing. He was a white cat—or would have been, but for an inexplicable fondness for the coal-bin. Steadfast in this partiality as in all his habits, he always, after his incursions into the black, took infinite pains to make amends. I wonder, by the way, how often you would bathe, if you had to do it with your tongue, as a cat does. Cats are obviously cleaner than dogs, although the latter, I admit, are more interesting, because of their very changefulness. Only the day before yesterday, at the foot of a small mountain which I was planning to ascend, a handsome dog, a young collie, came bounding to greet me. So enthusiastic was he that I could not keep his paws off my coat nor his tongue off my cheek. Yet I was a perfect stranger; he would have been just as appreciative of anybody else. And another day he might have tried to bite me. He accompanied me all the way up the mountain, by a very rough trail, and down again. Then, after an unsuccessful attempt to enter my car, he attached himself to another fortuitous wayfarer.

How different is a cat! Cats very seldom climb mountains, and they never do so in the company of unknown gentlemen. In fact, nothing short of intense personal devotion will move them to such unusual exercise. Yet the thing has happened. A cat of mine—not Moses, but a lady-cat, advanced in years, Sneezer by name—shared a mountain-climb with me. Quite new to the neighborhood of our summer cottage, she craved companionship; and when she saw the whole family starting forth for a walk she refused to stay in the house alone. Persuasions, even commands were of no avail. She stuck to us like a bond-peddler. For the first quarter or so she kept up the pace pretty well, ever and anon casting an anxious glance at her longer-legged fellow-climbers. Then she began to pant; and whenever she came to a smooth, moist rock, she would lie down on it to rest. Still she persisted, until we were half-way up. Then the poor old puss could go no further; outstretched on her cool stone she lay exhausted, looking up at me with despair in her eyes. I took her in my arms, where she lay in purring contentment until we reached the top. On the way down, she manifested some wonder and some apprehension, peering to and fro, but she made no move to leave her carrier, until we came in sight of the house. At that point, with a little cry of delighted recognition, she leaped from my arms, scurried to the cottage, and awaited us triumphantly at the door.

Proud of her prowess she was, no doubt. Both dogs and cats have a sense of self-respect; they are painfully conscious of humiliation, and resort to falsehood to save their faces. A cat, as everyone knows, is a skillful acrobat, and, however she may tumble, can nearly always land neatly on her feet. Nearly always, but not quite invariably. And when she does miss it and makes an awkward landing, her affectation of dignity is appalling. She will sit with her back to you, her shoulders hunched, her eyes half-closed, the picture of immobility, obviously trying to convince you that she has never budged. Only the nervous twitch of her tail-tip reveals the inner fire. A dog betrays false pride in a different way. Suppose you are traveling on a country road, and a dog rushes out at you with glistening teeth and homicidal mien, as so many of the arrogant creatures do. You speak to him with the tone of authority. A few dogs will nevertheless proceed with their attack; such beasts should be promptly killed, for they never can be cured. Most of the canine tribe, however, will desist on hearing the master's voice—every man being in principle the master of every dog. A simple-minded animal will either sink into surly silence or change his enmity to welcome, according to his temperament; but the shrewdly resourceful dog will begin sniffing about on the ground, as if he had come out into the road in search of something. Can duplicity go further?

The dog knows what mortification means; he knows the sting of mockery. Last week I passed a lawn where two dogs, a very large police dog and a very small Boston terrier, boon companions, are accustomed to disport themselves. There they were. But the police dog was enjoying a bone of unusual size and succulence, while the terrier (like Mother Hubbard's poor pet) had none. Perhaps not envious, but simply fascinated, the little fellow would draw slowly nearer and nearer; and when he came too close, his big friend would puff him away with a warning cough. After several repetitions of this act, the police dog evidently decided that it had gone on long enough. He picked up the bone, held it for a moment directly before the terrier's nose, waved it tauntingly to and fro, and then retired to eat it in peace.

A big and a little dog figure in the next story. But the contrast between them is much greater: a huge St. Bernard and a tiny black-and-tan. The scene is a wharf, with a lot of people wearily waiting. On a steamer's deck, well placed to watch, sits the narrator. The black-and-tan has evidently just broken away from his master; he is capering excitedly about, a string dangling from his neck. Spying the St. Bernard, he, in his uppishness, tries to tease the monster, charging at him with shrill barks again and again. At first the big brother pays no attention; then for a while gazes at the disturber with an air of contemptuous unconcern. Finally, when the annoyance has gone beyond all bounds, he grabs not the black-and-tan but the dependent cord; and, holding it firmly in his mouth, proceeds to drag the petty culprit round and round the wharf, before the eyes of the amused spectators, who instinctively form a ring. Frantic struggles, falsetto yelps are of no avail. Round and round goes the procession—the stately executioner and the agonized prisoner. At last the owner appears, to whom the St. Bernard courteously surrenders his captive, disgraced and penitent.

My own feeling toward dogs is curiously mixed. I love them and yet dread them. Somewhere else I have confessed the reason. When I was about three, a dog which I was caressing suddenly snapped and bit me through the lip. There is no mark of it on my face, but the mark on my mind is indelible. I suppose it was one of the greatest shocks of my life; for I adored animals, as children always do, and I must have had perfect faith in the nasty little brute. How powerfully our dispositions must be affected, not by the suppressed desires but by the overt happenings of childhood—trifles, often quite forgotten, phrases carelessly uttered by elders, as likely as not in jest!

Children are such solemn creatures, and so tena-

cious. Once I asked my mother for a cent, to attend
a show one of my playmates had announced. After
search in various places, she produced the coin, observing that it was her last penny. With a sinking
heart and a guilty feeling that has never quite left me,
I accepted the gift, being all on tiptoe to attend the
advertised performance—a trained cat. Rotten
enough the exhibition turned out to be. The youthful
Barnum simply placed his pet on the path in the back
yard, and bade us observe how still she sat. This she
did successfully enough, having previously declined
all invitations to jump over a string. And it was for
this (my conscience kept telling me) that I had reduced my mother to beggary. Such was the sorriest
show I ever witnessed, although I have seen many a
sad one since; and their sadness has always been intensified by that old sensation of guilt.

Among our frequent visitors was a large family of
children, who used to sit in a long row on the sofa and
scuff their feet. Having heard my mother playfully
remark that they were quite wearing out her carpet,
my filial devotion declared that something must be
done. So the next time the shuffling party was there
and the fricative process had begun, I walked along
the line and kicked each scraper vigorously in the
shins. As a social reform, this first attempt of mine
was so complete a failure as to discourage any subsequent efforts in that field. Too inarticulate to explain my moral purpose, I was set down as a pest—a

common fate of reformers! Even my mother, for whose sake the deed had been done, concurred in the opinion that my conduct was abominable; and acted in accordance with that conviction. Social evils may henceforth take care of themselves; nevermore shall they find an adversary in me.

That word "abominable": I recall distinctly where and when I first encountered it. 'Twas on a summer afternoon in the northeast corner of Franklin Square. The performer was a lady; I can still distinctly see her expression as she pronounced the word. She seemed to have a face especially designed for its utterance. In reality, her features may have been capable of conveying terror and pity; but the countenance engraved on my memory knows no catharsis save one of disgust. That is why I never say "abominable," myself; I have a deep-down fear of looking like her.

Speaking of abominations, I am inclined at the present moment to accord the palm to a new-fangled buckle. Were I Lord High Executioner, the inventor of that article should have a place near the top of my list, and the manufacturers, tailors and tradesmen who use it should come close after. Why, when mankind has had for centuries a perfectly good buckle, easy to do and undo, and absolutely sure in its grip— why, I repeat, should some enemy of his race come a-long with a contraption destitute of all these virtues? And how on earth could he persuade anyone to adopt it? Really, it is almost impossible nowadays to buy a genuine leather trunk-strap with a genuine old-fashioned buckle. What you get is a cloth band which stretches like molasses candy and wears out like paper; and, instead of a *bona fide* fastening, a Chinese puzzle over which you sweat and strain and curse, and which, when at last you think it is safe and the expressman has come for the trunk, slips away like an anchor on a smooth bottom. But the thing is at its worst when applied to a pair of knickerbockers. Down at your knees, where you cannot properly see nor conveniently reach, this devil's device is enough to drive a man to long trousers in mid-summer. Why should we submit to it? Has the spirit of the Tea Party quite forsaken us?

I suppose it has. To say that we are the most long-suffering people on earth is no news. We put up with more impositions, frauds, humbugs, and extortions than there are hours in the day. There is the publisher who sends you, unasked, a costly book, which you must either buy or go to the expense and trouble of returning. One chap, totally unknown to me, shipped me from New York a huge album valued at a hundred and fifty dollars. The only thing to do was to ship it back without opening the box. One never knows what legal vexation a rascally publisher plus a shyster lawyer may contrive. Still worse, because more frequent, is the new Blue Book of here, there, and everywhere; or the new Who's Who in Business, Who's Who in Beggary, or Who's Who in Jail. I don't mean, of course, the real *Who's Who* and *Who's Who in America*, but the fraudulent imitations, of weekly recurrence, which send insinuating circulars begging for your autobiography, and fatten on the fatuous vanity of simpletons who succumb. Let me confess. When I was a young man, I did (with some pains) furnish a paragraph to a peculiarly plausible exploiter, who signed a declaration to the effect that I thereby incurred no financial obligation. Shortly thereafter came a polite request for a portrait, which would add greatly to the interest of my very interesting biography. Well, I am ashamed to say I rummaged about until I unearthed a photograph, which I cut down to the required dimensions. The next move, as I might have known, was a gentle call for ten dollars to publish the illustration. At that, meek as I was, my spirit rose, and I called off the whole business.

The photographers, by the way, have a trick of their own. Every now and then you get from a reputable newspaper such a letter as this: inasmuch as the Press frequently needs the likeness of so prominent a public character, will you not be so kind as to sit for your picture—without expense to yourself—at Such and Such's Studio? Juvenile inexperience falls. You sit. The proofs arrive; they are very beautiful. At least, that is the opinion of the highly appreciative lady attendant who shows them to you. It would really be a pity of pities to lose so unique an opportunity. So you order a dozen for yourself. Vanity, vanity.

"We take pleasure in informing you that the Astrological Academy of Laputa, at its last meeting, elected you an Honorary Member." This is rather flattering to one not previously aware that his modest contributions to the science of Astrology had received more than local recognition. Alas! his self-satisfaction dwindles in proportion to the dues exacted of Honorary Members, and disappears entirely when he discovers that the Honorary Members are the only ones who pay anything at all.

Such thoughts as these give one a better opinion of dogs, which, delight as they may in barking and biting, do not elect one to Honorary Membership in the Society of Suckers. Innocent deceit, however, they may occasionally practice; perhaps harmless mischief. It was late in the afternoon, on a remote rural footway, that I felt a very gentle pressure against my side. Looking down, I saw a wolf's head projecting from under my arm. I shall doubtless win credence when I say that I was startled. There it was, only too plain, a great wolf's head sticking out between my arm and my body. What was one to do under such circumstances? Ought I to explain that I was carrying a basket of refreshments to my grandmother? That question was never answered, for the animal soon pulled its head out, gave me a quizzical glance, and, bounding away, revealed itself as a gigantic

police dog. Now, what I should like to know is this:
was the whole proceeding a practical joke? Or did
the beast steal up on me with hostile intent, and
then, finding that I smelled better than I looked, substitute a bit of amicable raillery? Who can tell me?

Some dogs think it great fun to run away—whether
impelled by mischief or by simple idiocy, I never
could make out. There was a nasty little dog belonging to M. LeBref. M. LeBref was not an artist, but he
was fond of paintings and painters, and, having no
occupation, was addicted to hanging about in
artists' studios; besides he was a great friend of my
teacher. We saw him, then, very often—him and his
diminutive dog. That winter I was spending my
leisure hours (when I had any) in trying to paint; and
for this purpose I used to frequent the shabby little
atelier of a painter at No. 7, Rue Chaptal; not a great
artist, perhaps, but an excellent teacher. It is not his
fault that my efforts met with small success. A pupil
of Yon, he exhibited regularly in the *salon*, and sold
some of his pictures, but he had to eke out his liveli-
hood by taking occasional disciples. There never
were many at a time. I recall Señor Rojas, a young
South American, with a keen eye for color but none
for form. And I remember an amusing little lady to
whom neither form nor color meant anything whatever; but she had (Heaven knows how) obtained a
post as governess in an English family, and, while
letting her bleached hair grow out dark, was per-

fecting herself in art. All sorts of people drifted in,
critics, artists, models, sociable acquaintances. For a
while we had a lame hawk which someone had bestowed on us, a poor broken-winged creature that
could fly no further than across the room. It grew
moderately tame. Occasionally it would perch just
behind me and inspect my work with that prolonged
and rigid intensity which characterizes its species;
then, after a spell of fearful silence, it would let out a
series of agonized screams and flutter feebly away. I
did not like that bird very well. It seemed prophetic,
somehow, of the Grand Guignol, which afterwards
came to inhabit that street.

I preferred the hawk, however, to M. Le Bref's dog.
Le Bref himself was all right, a friendly, fussy, precise, old-maidish, blond little man, with a shrill voice;
and that dog was the apple of his eye. Never but
once did he allow the animal out of his sight; but that
once was almost my undoing. For some reason which
I have forgotten, both he and my teacher were suddenly called away on an errand which did not admit
of canine companionship; and I was left alone in
charge of the sacred beast. Many and awful were the
injunctions I received; solemn were my promises.
How light a word is "responsibility," to describe the
weight that settled upon me when that studio door
was closed, with nobody within but the dog and me!
I tried to work; but how can a man paint when one
eye has to be riveted on a restless and stealthy little

demon? Soon I gave it up, and devoted myself un-
dividedly to guardianship. Holding the creature in
my lap was out of the question, he struggled so; and
I had nothing to tie him with. We sat, then, on
opposite sides of the room, in hostile watchfulness.
Thus two deadly foes, prisoners in the same cell, may
glower at each other. A knock on the door! Without
waiting for an answer, the miserable knocker opens
the door a crack, to drop a package inside. That
crack is enough. Through it, like an electric current
traveling at the speed of light, darts the accursed pet;
and through that door I plunge in pursuit, hatless,
clad in my painting smock. On a fair straightaway I
believe I could have beaten that dog. But I could not
dodge between people's legs nor so easily project myself through a crowd. Down the Rue Chaptal we ran,
around the corner into the next street (whose name
I can almost remember), on and on, now this way,
now that, but in general bearing to the eastward. Our
race aroused an interest that was almost Olympic;
and I am pleased to recall that in those prehistoric
days public sympathy favored the American competitor. To that sympathy I owe in some measure my
victory. As we approach Notre Dame de Lorette, a
timely interference arrests the fugitive for half a
second. Swifter than thought, I pounce upon him and
grip him with ruthless claws. Of what avail now are
squeals and scratches? Smock-clad, bare-headed,
disheveled, red, but triumphant, I rush him back to

his prison-house, where we luckily arrive just before the return of his master. Of our mad escapade neither the dog nor I ever breathed a word.

That studio life was an experiment; and never, I believe, did experimenter get more pleasure from an unsuccessful venture. Everything about it was a delight: the mysteries of the palette, the daubs on my clothes, the smell of turpentine, the purchase of paints at the *maison de couleurs*. Almost too heavenly to speak of were those excursions into the Bois, or to really rustic scenes with riverside and willows, when the advancing season and my advancing technique made such things possible. But even the still life compositions in the *atelier* were full of excitement. For one of them—a dessert piece—we needed a bottle of champagne, which (not finding it among our properties) Rojas and I procured at a cost of two francs; and when our pictures were done, after a week's toil in the hot room, we opened the tepid bottle and gaily drank the contents to the health of "the master."

Unsuccessful, to be sure, the experiment was, but not altogether unjustifiable; for I still believe that I naturally see things from the painter's rather than the narrator's point of view. My novel-writing friends tell me that when they look at the people about them, for instance in the subway, they instinctively interpret the faces and figures in terms of character; and so do I. But when they proceed to affirm that the next stage is a story which takes shape all of its own

accord, I part company with them; for me the inevitable sequence is a study of lines and values and
colors by which the character in question (if one
were really an artist) might be expressed.

Twenty is an experimental age. On the whole, I do
not envy those (if such there be) whose first experiment is so satisfactory that they make no other. I am
not sorry that in those decorative days, following the
picturesque habit of Parisian students, I wore a shock
of black hair and a little two-pointed beard, like a
brigand in comic opera. In fact, I subsequently discovered that my hirsute adornment had won for me
the nickname of "l'Espagnol" in M. Roland's
dancing classes. That was another experiment. M.
Roland had a large Terpsichorean school on the Rue
Royale, next door but one to the house which in later
years became "Maxim's." The master was a comely
blond gentleman of thirty or so, accomplished and
well-bred, a good linguist, something of a composer—
I recall a piece of his called *The Roland Quick-Step*. By
profession he was *premier danseur* at the Opéra.

Painting, dancing—and music? Yes, a very feeble
stab. But that was in Siena. In those days Siena lay
well outside the tourist's zone, and was much closer
to the thirteenth century than to the twentieth. A
negro, appearing one day on the streets, attracted as
much attention as a circus parade; on all hands arose
a wondering cry of "il moro, il moro!" We had a
circus once—a very good one—in the theatre on the

Lizza. Of course there was no menagerie—nothing but acrobatic and equestrian stunts; and the small size of the company obliged one man to play many parts. That performer of international identity who, standing on a cantering horse, removes one set of garments after another, here finally revealed himself in a red shirt as "il Garibaldino," to the intense patriotic delight of the audience. The leading artist, poor man, really had too much to do. Twice he missed fire in his principal act. Whereupon he sat down in despair and had a good cry; after which he bravely took up arms again, and his third trial met with the proverbial result. At that same Lizza theatre we had a dramatic company, which gave a thrilling play on Galileo, called *Eppur si move*, and a melodrama, *la Ladra di tre milioni*, with a part for the traditional improvising Stenterello. My neighbor at the latter show could not be reconciled to the lack of personal charm in the heroine. "Non ha niente di bello quella donna, è propio brutta," he would repeat in a tone of gentle but profound disappointment, with a singular drawl which reminded me of some of our rural speakers in the South. When I afterwards tried to imitate him to my Sienese friends, they told me he must have come from Val di Chiana.

Neither was beauty a conspicuous trait in our operatic choruses. For we had an opera season, on the more aristocratic stage of the City Hall. I purchased a season ticket, which consisted of a ten-inch iron key

to my box, but I generally preferred the front row of
the pit. In the repertory were some pieces which one
knows by name but very seldom has a chance to
hear—*Maria di Rohan*, for instance, and *I Lombardi*, a
chorus from which I used to sing at school. The
prima donna was a pretty enough young woman,
with a thin little voice, and no tiniest notion of acting.
Her husband, the tenor, was pretty, too, and quite
devoid of histrionic intention. He was one of those
dreadful squealing tenors—*tenorini*—who so get on
one's nerves. The public stood him as long it could;
then, after four or five performances, solemnly decided that he must be hissed (or rather whistled, for
whistling is the sign of disapproval in Latin lands).
This verdict having been reached, the sentence was
executed with great thoroughness; and the unfortunate tenor had a fit. The baritone was the only
tolerable member of the troup. It is hard to believe
how totally absent, in old-fashioned Italian opera,
was any attempt at illusion. I remember seeing on the
grand stage of San Carlo, in Naples, the blind beggar-
woman of *La Gioconda* all a-glitter with diamonds and
trailing after her a magnificent silk train. Yet forty
years later, on the same boards, I saw *La Traviata*
given with all the dramatic effectiveness of a performance at the Comédie Française.

But I started to speak of the Sienese chorus. In
those days (possibly it is the same now) wandering
companies did not transport their chorus with them;

they recruited one in each town. Now, for some
reason it was thought highly improper for any decent
young woman to sing in an operatic chorus. The
recruits, then, had to be culled from those whom age
and nature had made as safe as Caesar's wife. For
this particular season we had a female assembly of
eight, who possessed among them a total of four
teeth, if my count was correct. When they first
appeared behind the footlights, a humorist in the
gallery shouted: "O bbelle fanciulle! bbelle!" And
even the musicians had to stop tooting and join in the
general merriment. After all, the choristers on the
stage mattered little; for the audience sang all the
choruses, and sang them well. Everybody in town,
apparently, could sing better than the professionals.
Late in the evening, groups of men would gather in
the streets and arrange part songs. One thought of the
England of the times of Samuel Pepys.

Wooden ploughs carried one back still further. And
lamps! they were exactly like the ones the ancient
Romans used—gravy dishes with a wick in the spout.
Diligent search was needed to find one kerosene
luminary of modern type. I really needed it, for
reading. Most of the people, I fancy, were satisfied
with a very moderate amount of bookishness. A law
student was among my acquaintances, an amiable
youth named Camillo (I have forgotten his last
name); but his room never knew a book. Siena really
had a University. A young professor of law, who

sometimes used to call at our house, was Enrico
Ferri, later a famous parliamentarian and socialist
leader. Vivacious and brilliant he was, thoroughly
attractive, already imbued with humanitarian principles and convinced that crime is a disease. Another
visitor was my Italian teacher, Father Conti, of gruff
and grumpy exterior, and mumbly in his speech. A
good man, though, and a helpful guide. A pioneer
in kindergarten work in Italy, he had at his house a
giardino-scuola for little boys. He had asked to be
relieved of a parish, he told me, because it upset him
so to be called to the dying. Three horrors he had:
the moribund, the French, and the fireplace. A fire
in his room always gave him a headache; when the
cold became unendurable, he would go to bed—but
fire was never to be mentioned. And how he did hate
France! My landlord, the Cavaliere Ignazio Gati, an
anticlerical, would have preferred not to have a
priest coming into his house; but he politely made no
objection. The Cavaliere, a tall, thin, tubercular
veteran of the War of Liberation, was the bookseller
of the town, and, as befits a bookseller, a man of some
reading and much intelligence, combining habitual
abstemiousness with excellent taste in volumes, wines,
and dainties.

I am glad to have known Siena when it was absolutely unspoiled. The few English people who lived
there simply blended into the background. Now there
are suburbs, automobiles, electric lights, an absurd

trolley-car serpentining through the main street, and a water supply, for which the citizens had been hunting since Dante's day. Even these things almost blend; and the tourists do not yet outnumber the natives. But the absolute harmony is gone. It is good to have known the old Ghibelline city when, still proud of Montaperti, she perched on her hilltop, with her narrow crooked streets picturesque with hunchbacks and broad-hatted peasant women, blocked now and then from side to side by a yoke of long-horned white oxen; with her staid architecture and her amazing cathedral of black and white marble; with her outlook over rolling farms and brooks and hog-back bridges, and, in the distance, the Apennines and grand old Mont' Ammiata.

There it was that I was moved to take singing lessons. All this, I admit, has not much to do with dogs—save that a bad singer is in that region called a *cane*. Anyhow, dog or no dog, I found an upright piano to let; I believe the cost was about a dollar a month, including transportation. It is curious, by the way, that we have come to call a *pianoforte*, or "soft-loud" (an instrument with pedals), simply *piano*; just as the *opera in musica*, or "work in music," is reduced to *opera*; and *piccolo flauto*, or "little flute" to *piccolo*.

A music-teacher, too, I discovered, a young pianist, who, although he had even less voice than I, had in Milan acquired the Lamperti method of vocal instruction and was induced to make an attempt

with the boy barbarian from America. It must have
been a trying experience for him; for me, however
severe, it was enlightening and full of excitement.
After a few months he proposed that we should pay
a visit to his patroness, the old Countess Tolomei,
who lived alone in the grim Palazzo of that name in
the heart of the city. She had been, in her youth, an
operatic star in Paris. To her I was to sing, and she
was to criticize my vocalics and name my voice.
Really, I suppose, I was taken as an exhibit, an
offering from a grateful *protégé* to a benignant power.
Benignant though her heart might be, however, I
was warned that she could be terrible, if musically
offended. Again and again my instructor, Signor
Lapi, adjured me to stick to my notes and not fall
into unintended improvisation. If I should sing out of
tune, as I too frequently did, especially if I should
sharp (my besetting sin), the Countess was capable
in her fury, of throwing at my head any object, light
or heavy, that might be within reach. Thus encouraged, I accompanied Signor Lapi, with throb-
bing heart, to the dread trial. Two things, at the
very start, gave me vast relief: first, the patroness's
unmistakably kind reception; second, a swift observation that no portable furniture of damaging possibilities lay in her immediate neighborhood. Indeed,
in the confused elation of that moment I blundered
into some happy phrase. I cannot tell what' it was (it
surely had nothing to do with *la Pia*); but it im-

mensely pleased our hostess, who during the whole
interview was graciousness and indulgence personi-
fied. She played my accompaniments, while I
executed the songs so carefully rehearsed with my
teacher. I think they were *Sognai* and *Le Ninfee*.
Thanks to her appreciation, I sang far less badly than
ever before (or since). Signor Lapi gazed at me with a
wonder that bordered on incredulity. My voice, the
Countess declared, was a *basso centrale*, and *molto
simpatica*. With a few friendly and expert suggestions,
she urged me to persevere, and warmly congratulated
my professor, whose thin face beamed with unwonted
satisfaction. Then she lapsed into French, evidently
glad of an opportunity to revive that once familiar
language. And that was the climax of my musical
career.

Yes, I am glad to have tried all these funny experiments. They did me good, I fancy, because I did not
at the time take any of them too seriously; they were
pastimes, nothing more. I worked as hard over them
as I ever worked at anything, but I did not worry—
that is, not really worry, as one does over one's bread-
winning business. So they were happy experiences
and they remain as happy memories. And I learned
something from every one. I acquired an appreciation of painting and of music, which, not having
been born to the arts, I should not have had otherwise. For dancing and for hirsute eccentricities I got
at least a certain degree of tolerance.

Not so happy is my recollection of an equestrian experiment in Heidelberg. As a small boy, my country life had included some horseback riding; but I must have been a very small boy indeed. It surely fell in the year of the Franco-Prussian war, for I remember a farmer remarking to my father (who was with me) that he ought to send me over to France as a cavalry officer; and when my father raised the objection that my legs were too short, the rustic retorted that Napoleon III had short legs, too. All this had sunk into the remote past when, at the age of twenty-one, I found myself spending a summer in Heidelberg. I had graduated from Harvard the year before. The other two boys, Walter G. and Billy H., were still students at Tech; but we were all of us about of an age, and all of us ready for adventure. Those evenings of band concert and beer, up in the garden of the famous old castle, seemed to us, at that time of life, full of romance. They were indeed teeming with uncertainty. Which of us three was it really who fell under the table that night? We never could reach an agreement, at least, the other two (who seemed to have conspired) never agreed with me. Then there used to be a plausible Italian candy-vendor, who would come around after ten o'clock, when people's brains were at not their sharpest, and propose at each table a little game. A tiny bag of gum drops was the stake. The Italian was to think of a number, and each of us was to try to guess it; if we

guessed right, we got the gum drops for nothing; if
our guess was wrong, we paid fifty pfennigs, or whatever the price was. Luck somehow invariably smiled
on the seller. It was a game to which the maxim
caveat emptor was peculiarly applicable. Yet hope
always beckoned. Thus, little by little, we would
ease ourselves of coin and fill ourselves up with gum
drops. Now, it was gum drops rather than beer (on
this point we were unanimous) which was responsible
for the subtabular disappearance of—but I am not
going to tell whether it was Billy or Walter.

Those two lads had too much pocket-money. One
of their extravagances was the purchase of two
beautifully carved meerschaum pipes, wherewith to
excite the envy of the people at home. It occurred to
them, however, that the maximum of concupiscence
would not be aroused unless the bowls were colored;
and they knew that the only way to color a meerschaum is to smoke it. Thus far all appeared simple.
In theory, to be sure, it was plain enough; but practice speedily brought the discovery that pipe-smoking
meets with violent protest from the unaccustomed
stomach. And Billy's stomach and Walter's stomach
were equally contumacious in their refusal to become
accustomed. Failure seemed inevitable. Did they
despair? Not in vain were they students of science.
The technical ingenuity won by three years of the
Institute at last found a way. A couple of pairs of
bellows, some rubber tubing, a box of cigars, un-

limited patience, and the thing was done. Cigars, because it was found that for some reason smoking-tobacco would not stay alight. Patience, because the coloring process proved to be unexpectedly slow; in fact, with the best of intention, one could detect scarcely any progress from week to week. Undeterred, however, they would sit hour by hour at their two windows (which looked out on the Anlage) working the bellows and pumping forth clouds of smoke. For our amiable landlady, Frau P., found herself obliged to prohibit ductless fumigation. No wonder: because the two vicarious smokers argued that, inasmuch as their engines and not they had all the enjoyment of the vice, they might as well economize by using the cheapest possible cigars. The enjoyment, whoever had it, came to a close. A sudden and fatal catastrophe cut off the hope that was still hoping. One day a great commotion was heard in the street, a great clatter of great wagons, a loud ring at the door-bell; and the Heidelberg Fire Department, aroused by the continuous outpour of smoke during the last month, stood fully uniformed in the front entry, ready to do or die. They did.

This diversion having found a sad quietus, it behooved us to turn our fertile invention to something else. "How would it do," said Billy, "to take a horse-back ride?" Now, Billy really was a good rider, having been for years the proprietor of a pony. Walter was nearly as inexperienced as I. Neither

Walter nor I, however, wished to confess incompetence; we confined ourselves to skepticism as to the procurability of saddle-horses, a seemingly safe and reasonable doubt. But the resourceful Billy was equal to the occasion. At a livery stable, nearly across the way, he unearthed equestrian equipment and three steeds which, despite a suspicious suggestion of the cab, were declared by the owner to be primarily destined for the saddle. He warned us, indeed, not to give too free rein to their turbulent impetuosity. We had decided to ride up along the Neckar to the Schwalbennest, a picturesque little ruin on the summit of a rock by the riverside. Bright was the sun and calm the air when we set forth, not without considerable urging of our reluctant mounts. I fancy we never should have got out of town, had not Billy, who surely must have had a better horse than Walter or I, contrived to inspire in that creature the idea of a pace faster than a walk; and the other two animals followed. I would not give the impression that our gait at any time was rapid. Walter's steed, to be sure, if touched with a whip, would leap into the air, with a forward lunge, as if to annihilate space, but as soon as he landed on his feet would resume his habitual hearse-like pace. My own horse, whose main desire in life, apparently, was to scratch himself, had developed the trick of walking and at the same time leaning against a wall; so successfully did he practice this art that he scraped all the skin off the knuckles of my right hand. Happily there were no walls on the left side of the road. Regardless of traffic rules (there being no traffic), I tried to keep the beast on that quarter, but in vain. Instead, he would almost trot whenever he espied a good rough wall ahead, so eager was he to rub himself and me against it. My right leg was reduced to a state of numb indifference. Except for the walls, the landscape was rather pretty, and the ride had its interesting features. As we passed through a village, the inhabitants would all pour out and stare at us, apparently never having seen civilians on horseback before. Nearly all were afflicted with goitre, which gave them an uncanny, vacant look; we seemed to be riding through a crowd of goblins. The Schwalbennest, our attractive goal, was eventually reached. We all rode up the steep, crumbly path to the summit, but Walter and I preferred to lead our horses down. The ride home, though increasingly painful to inexpert sitters, was uneventful until we reached the confines of the little city. Then the steeds scented the stable; and all the unused speed which had accumulated during the day was expended in a wild dash through the whole length of the Anlage. Nothing could hold them—that is, Walter's and mine. Billy managed it somehow. We, helpless and terrified two, went whistling through the air, hatless, coattails flying horizontal behind us, to the amazement of the promenaders, who evidently thought we were engaged in a mad race. Walter and

I arrived neck and neck, while Billy came in at a comparatively dignified pace some moments after. That evening at table, Frau P. congratulated the two John Gilpins on their spirited performance, and considerately deplored poor Mr. H's defeat, which, she sympathetically added, must have been the fault of a poorer horse.

Dear Old Heidelberg, *Stadt fröhlicher Gesellen*, finest of towns on Rhine and Neckar! We had met long before, when I was thirteen. The Villa Bergheim was then my abode, a capacious boarding-house on the southern outskirts of the city, at the opposite end from the Castle. It was kept, and well kept, by the wife of an invalid retired Professor, whose paralytic legs required a wheelchair. They had, I think, some English relations; at any rate, their very beautiful blond daughter, during my stay, was married to an English officer. The boarders were nearly all British. Numerous elderly ladies played bézique in the evening; and I acquired that game. Younger misses and the young men often indulged in mild sports—not in the small winter parlor at the front, but in the long dining-room or, as the season progressed, in the summer drawing-room with great glass doors opening on a garden which stretched in two levels, with walks and arbors, to the high wall beside the railway track.

There it was that the boys played a trick on me. One of them challenged me to a footrace of ten laps around the oval walk. Proud of my prowess as a

runner, I accepted—only to discover (I think at the
eighth lap) the plurality of my competitor; for the
rascals were relaying one another at each round. In
that garden, near the house, there was a game called
"the pole," wherein we little lads were allowed to
join the young gentlemen. The apparatus consisted of
a telegraph pole, or something of the sort, about
twenty feet long, horizontally supported by two
trestles at some three feet above the ground. We
chose sides. Mounting on that precarious bridge from
opposite ends, we then would rush each other, the
leader of each party trying to bump his opponent off.
As one or the other fell, he ran around to the end and
clambered up in the rear, and the next in line took
his place at the head. Victory consisted in one side
sweeping the log clear of its adversaries. Hands were
not to be used, either for offense or for defense. It
was exciting sport. I learned, by the way, that in
stating rules one said, not "mustn't," but "mayn't."
Moreover, in such games as tag and hide-and-seek
the protagonist is not "it" but "he." As an American,
I was promptly nicknamed "Stranger," that being
regarded as our national form of address; and
"Stranger" I remained to the end.

They treated me pretty well, though—especially
Charley, my namesake, a plump, humorous boy,
serviceable in preventing active hostility whenever
my impertinence and Reggie's ill temper were on the
point of striking fire. Reggie did give me one day a

most sanguinary nose. As I look back at it, I cannot say I greatly blame him; but at the time my apparently unquenchable bloodshed seemed a tragic outrage. I should like to see him try it now. His four years' seniority, once so helpful, would be anything but an advantage today. I never really liked him; neither did Charley, who was more inclined to side with me, in spite of national prejudice. A thin, quick lad was Reggie, dark, fitful, and unpredictable. He had two brothers: John, a grown-up man with a mustache, eighteen if he was a day, and inexplicably good to me; concerning Rafie, the youngest, I can say only that the minor brothers of one's playmates are always objectionable.

It was on the Neckar, under the tutelage of John, Reggie, and Charley, that I first learned to row. In consideration of Britannia's ruling the wave, it was to be assumed that every English boy was a born boatman. We obtained a four-oared shell, with the appropriate four sculls, and practised ourselves nearly into perfection. "Why, man, we're teaching you your life!" cried the sometimes melodramatic Reggie. When, in later years, I have looked upon that shallow stream, impetuous in current and full of rocks and eddies, it has been an amazement to me that we did not learn death. Having escaped, we were doubtless thenceforth immune.

More successful as an oarsman than as an equestrian, I once, in middle life, won a second prize in a boat-race. It was a fishermen's race, off Duxbury Beach, and there were money prizes; but, thanks to the violent wind, entrants were fewer than had been expected. To tell the truth, when I put off from shore that day in my dory, it was not to compete, but to pick up any unfortunates who might be upset; for I knew none of the fishermen could swim. As I approached the judges' boat, however, they roared instructions at me through a megaphone, evidently assuming that I was in the game; and I did not like to disappoint them. Not much that the judges had bellowed had been audible to me in the gale; hence it came about that I supposed the course to be considerably longer than it was, and rowed a good bit further than the others. I broke an oar, too, a good ash oar; but I always carried a spare one. When at last I came alongside the judicial craft again, a pistol rang forth, a judge leaned far out over the side, with something in his hand. I approached as close as I could in that sea without smashing myself up, and leaned out also. There remained in my clutch a two-dollar bill. And thus I became a professional oarsman. It has always been my belief that had I not mistaken the length of the course, by winning the first prize instead of the second I should not have sold my amateur status so cheap. That is what comes of not knowing one's goal.

Why is it that in our childhood we always said "ghouls" instead of "goal?" Even if our playgrounds were as ghoul-haunted as the woodland of Weir, how are we to account for the *s* ? Is it the same serpent-like ending that fastens itself to "a woods," "a works," "a links?" And is that, in turn, the same *s* that clings to "I'd just as livs" for "just as lief?" A similar super-fluous sibilant adorned such phrases as "no fairs," "findin's keepin's," and "makin's up bein's it." The last monstrosity, by the way, signifies that the pro-poser of a sport shall therein play the title rôle. It was as hard for us to get away from that *s* as it would be for a disciple of Mencken to write a sentence without the word "obscene." Labor as they may, the word comes popping in, like Charles the First's head in Mr. Dick's memorial.

Words and phrases and rhythms possess us. A German friend of mine, who had mastered English well, was continually ejaculating "Great Caesar's ghost!" After some years of pondering, I constructed a satisfactory theory to account for his choice of this particular exclamation for his pet expletive. He needed something to replace "Du lieber Gott," which shadowed him as "obscene" shadows the Menckenist; and "Great Caesar's ghost" has exactly the same movement—not to speak of the identity of the conspicuous second vowel and the quasi-identity of the final word.

There was a time when, in the Harvard Faculty of Arts and Sciences, it was impossible for any debater (and we debated everlastingly) to begin his objection otherwise than "I fail to understand . . ." One day, having quit a meeting in the middle, I went out for a breath of stillness, and met Josiah Royce in the Yard. "What are they doing in there," he asked, "failing to understand?"

A fail-to-understand complex. A waitress in a Boston railway restaurant had been putting up patiently with a lot of complaint from a querulous customer. When the censorious female had departed, a lady at a neighboring table expressed her sympathy. "Well, it's pretty fierce," admitted the waitress. "But after all, the find-fault complex ain't so bad. What gets my goat is the got-to-get-a-train complex."

How true it is that there are always two sides to the shield! One and the same word may blow hot or cold according to the point of view. As you approach the glass door of that same eating-house, you see painted thereon a touching expression of devotion and self-immolation, *tuo*, "thine." But looked at from the inside of the glass, on your departure, the loving "tuo" becomes the inhospitable monosyllable, "out." It is all a matter of association. Before I ever had the pleasure of meeting that genial, bushy-haired scholar, Professor Calvin Thomas, I had in my mind a distinct picture of him as a completely bald-headed gentleman, like Bill Nye—all from the suggestion of the etymon of his given name. And I shall never cease to regard that war-time diplomat, Boy-Ed, as a shocking example of juvenile depravity.

The word depravity brings me, with a jerk, back to my subject, which, if I remember aright, was Dogs. It now behoves me to record an incident in which dogs and depravity shall be connected more intimately than by a chance alliteration. That, to my sorrow, I can easily do. In wintertime I am fond of wandering across-country over the snowy hills. Late one afternoon I come upon an abandoned house. Paint has vanished, shutters are falling to pieces, every pane is shattered. Beyond is a tumbledown wall surmounted (rather curiously) by a barbed wire fence. On one side, in better repair than the dwelling, is a long henhouse, from which emerges a substantial smokestack. One sign of life there is: two black dogs are playing in the yard. At my approach, the animals suddenly stop their innocent sport and with a savage snarl rush at me. Vain are my protests. One rends my trousers, the other tears a great hole in my sleeve. While they crouch, glaring, ready for another spring, a dark, untidy woman appears at the door of the old house and addresses them in a strange tongue. Reluctantly they hold in a bit. Taking advantage of the opportunity, but not daring to avert my eyes, I back toward the ruined wall. They follow slowly but ominously. I remember the barbed wire, which cannot be climbed backward, nor swiftly. Then I bethink me of my profession, and thank my stars that I am not a boatman, a rider, a dancer, a singer, a painter, but a lecturer. Closing my heart to pity, I lectured those two dogs. I lectured them long and hard, and my words went home. Consternation, contrition, entreaty succeeded one another in the canine faces. They lay on their bellies and whined piteously, trying apparently to drag themselves near enough to lick my hand. This was the moment. Over the fence I went, leaving behind me forever the sylvan still and its lawless guardians.

I am convinced, after all, that my selection of a calling was for the best. That conviction is corroborated by another adventure, in which the canine element appears to better advantage. I am invited to give an address on a solemn occasion at a thriving and justly famous country college. At the station I am met by a friendly professor and driven some miles over the snow to the model College Inn. Kind hosts escort me over the grounds. It is a wonderfully beautiful place. In the midst of all my admiration, I am struck by the abundance of dogs. There must be at least one for every inhabitant. "Yes," is the reply. "We love dogs here. Nothing is closed to them. Why, they often walk into the hall where you are to speak this evening. Only last Tuesday, while Mr. Snodgrass, whom we had secured at considerable expense, was reading us his latest and most beautiful poem, just as he reached the climax for which he had made such artistic preparation, a dog fight broke out in the back of the room and not a word was audible." That gives me food for thought. As I enter the hall at eight o'clock, I gaze about me with a happy smile on my lips but with apprehension in my heart. A rapid survey discloses no dog as yet. I begin. Hardly have I reached "thirdly," when a Great Dane appears majestic in the central doorway. With stately slowness he marches down the middle aisle. It so happens that I am right in the midst of some noble sentiments about animals and particularly dogs. I try not to notice the all too appropriate advent of an exemplar, and talk steadily on, with no more quaver in my voice than the subject justifies. One heavy paw after another thuds on the steps; the kingly creature takes his place on the platform and sits down beside me. I have just reached the peak of my enthusiastic encomium of his kind. With one hand resting on his head I deliver the ringing words, and the audience responds. The Great Dane and I could not have played it better had we rehearsed it for a month. Thereupon he lay down at my feet, where he quietly remained until the speech was over.

Do you wonder that I regard the dog with mixed feelings? And that I associate him with the choice of a profession?

INDIANA PLACE

THE first tribute of reader to author is sympathy. Since my recent lament over the disappearance of Indiana Place, goal of my childish church-going, I have received from three sympathetic readers the consoling assurance that the old Place still exists—no longer a Place, to be sure, but a Street, Corning by name. To Corning Street, then, I betook myself, eager to verify or to disprove. I believe they are right. Wherefore the title, Corning, I cannot conjecture; but the change from Place to Street is obviously due to the extension of Shawmut Avenue into Tremont Street, cutting off the end of the once secluded and issueless pocketway, and perhaps engulfing the old chapel eventually in the great Morgan Memorial. The location is right, just beside the railway tracks. Unaltered in architecture are the uniform, low, flat brick houses. Yet how transformed! Every one of them now bears a notice, "Rooms to let." Such is the demand for these signs that they are evidently turned out wholesale on a standardized model, and the labels are as uniform as the dwellings they adorn. Despite this suggestion of depopulation, the road is full of children at play. Among them I

saw two little girls with the most gorgeous crop of
outstanding red hair that ever greeted my eyes; the
older one especially (they were surely sisters), a lass
of eleven or so, with a broader halo to frame her
delicate face, resembled nothing so much as a great
golden sunset. Aside from these cherubic figures,
there was no suggestion of anything ecclesiastical.
Quite the contrary. Altogether unchurchlike is that
decorative young woman who emerges from one of
the doors and steps down the street, revealing—thanks
to the high visibility afforded by much wind and
little raiment—a nautical design in tattoo on either
thigh. It is no wonder that my unaided efforts had
failed to identify Corning Street with Indiana Place.

Even churches in that quarter are unchurched.
There is the Berkeley Street Church, the one nearly
at the corner of Tremont, now a Scenic Auditorium—
devoted, I gather, to almost every pursuit except
worship. It still flaunts, however, its preposterous
brown steeple, a composite of meaningless incon-
gruous curves. I wish I could describe that steeple.
My father, rather a serious person, never could see it,
or even think of it, without bursting into a paroxysm
of laughter. That was always a bit annoying to my
Uncle B. You see my Uncle B. was a deacon of the
shrine in question and, although he could not un-
reservedly approve of its style, he felt himself in
loyalty bound to defend it from excessive derision.

Old Florence has nothing to match that sanctuary.

Nor, indeed is anything in Boston quite like anything in Florence—not even that engine-house on the
East Side which has copied the tower of the Palazzo
Vecchio. Yet, all the same, when you look down on
the Hub City from Parker Hill, if the day and the
hour are just right, you can almost fancy yourself on
the heights of San Miniato. You need distance; you
need the proper light, a combination of warm glow
and hazy indistinctness; you need above all (I confess it) imagination. Granted these conditions, you
get something which perhaps is not Florence, but is
suggestive of Florentine charm; for you have color,
you have an old-world tangle of streets, a curving
streak of water, a rim of hills. Too modern? Even the
Tuscan city renews itself. I can remember the Mer-
cato Vecchio when it really was "vecchio," ere it was
rescued from "secolare squallore," according to the
inscription composed (it is said) by dear old Senator
Del Lungo. Boston, too, has seen aged markets fade
away. There was the Boylston Market, and the Dover
Market. The latter was turned into a cheap show-
house, then into a Yiddish theater. The former, the
ancient Boylston, where on School Parade days we
used to gather with our freshly furbished Civil War
muskets, is now displaced by a great clothing establishment. Near by, Barnum once had a museum. I
remember seeing there an apelike animal described
as a "young gorilla," which, when you gave it a bit of
sugar, would perch the morsel on its under lip, ex-

tending that support far enough to the fore to assure a good inspection, before it ventured to admit the delicacy into its mouth. Perhaps, after all, it really was a young gorilla; at any rate, it was young.

Young by comparison with Boylston and Dover is the still active (though unmarketed) Washington Market. How people shook their heads when it was built! Sheer madness, they said, to expect business so far up town, beyond West Chester Park. I have not been inside it for fifty years, and cannot say whether it ever accumulated a genuine market smell. A short distance from it, due west, however, on Shawmut Avenue, I recently effected an entrance that took me by surprise. I thought I knew that neighborhood pretty well, having once lived on the corner of West Chester Park and Shawmut Avenue; but I did not know all. Strolling briskly and carelessly along, on a southerly course, I became vaguely conscious of having passed on my right a mysterious opening—a little driveway through the ground floor of a brick block. That seemed to demand investigation. So I turned back, crossed the street, and penetrated. Fully persuaded that all that section of the city was solidly filled up, I almost rubbed my eyes when I emerged into a great open quadrangle bathed in sunshine. At the further end, rather dim in the distance, were the houses of another street. Right and left were the rear parts of dwellings, those on the right flanked by little back yards, while on the left the board fences were falling away and the individual yards were merging into the central area. Like banners on a festal day, countless strings of undergarments flutteringly enlivened the dull brick walls. But the great central space; was it empty? Far from it. A home for the aged, a receptacle for the infirm, it was a vast repository for decrepit automobiles. Fords, Chevrolets, Dodges, Nashes, Buicks, stood in silent, patient rows, awaiting their gradual dissolution. Some looked almost usable, some had lost a vital part, some were generally shattered, some were in so advanced a stage of decomposition as to have lost all semblance to their former selves. And there was still room for many more. Whence came all these invalids, and what was ultimately to be their fate? Who can tell? It was not a hospital; better were it called a city of the dead. Yet some of the inmates seemed to retain a spark of life. One could only wish them a quick and painless end. O for an Andersen, to lend a voice to the poor lingerers, to translate to us their thoughts, their recollections, their whispered secrets! What a sequence of interesting tales could be revealed—a thousand and one flivveries! But to the prosy intruder they confided nothing. He could only turn his back and pass on.

From the Court of Cars it is no long passage to that dismal region between Tremont Street and Shawmut Avenue where lurks the Secret Square. This is probably not its real name, but I have so christened it for lack of an official designation. Nowhere around its perimeter have I been able to detect its lawful title. There are signs, to be sure, but they tell only the names of the debouching streets. By a strange fatality (or was it design?) these all begin with *W*—Weston, Williams, Westminster, Warwick. It is a fairly big square, built around a quadrilateral park of incomprehensible shabbiness. Sprinkled with unhealthy trees, it was once covered—or meant to be covered—with greensward, but the grass is nearly all trodden away. One suspects a high birthrate in the quarter, although for the moment no children are to be seen. Perhaps all the grass-treaders have died. Indeed, there is a curious lifelessness in all the scene, despite the openness, the low sky-line, the sunlight—a desolation, a suggestion of blight. No wonder the square prefers to remain anonymous. It was evidently planned at the time when American architecture was at its lowest ebb. Cheap and pretentious these buildings were when they were new. On the four sides may be found examples of all the most fantastically bad types of construction. The far side in particular—once certainly the glory of the neighborhood—ought to be preserved in a museum of horrors. A row of ill-shaped houses fronted with a thin veneer of marble and profusely decorated with ugly colors and uglier designs. Foundations sagging, walls opening in cracks, marble veneer scaling off here and there, they are apparently still inhabited, and still maintain a certain fatuous swagger. I noticed a plentitude of physician's shingles. Can they minister to mental mouldiness? Indeed, are they, themselves, really alive; or have they, one by one, followed their patients into the other world? One can almost see them, rigid, desiccated corpses, sitting dusty behind the dirty window-panes.

Suddenly it occurs to me that I have seen all this before. Not in a dream, not in some previous existence, but in my waking boyhood. Yes, I remember now: I visited this spot with my father, when these artistic creations were taking shape. And my father, with uncanny foreknowledge, predicted that the piles would sink, the walls would droop and break open, the marble facing would peel. He was always interested in construction, expert in judgment of soil, material, and plan; and he liked to take me to look at new buildings in process of erection. When he was a lad (he told me once), he was so fascinated in watching the progress of Girard College, then going up in Philadelphia, that he spent more than one night on a marble slab beside the walls. I fancy he came near being an architect; and so, at one period, did I. The urge did not find satisfaction until the third generation.

In my earliest walking years my father and I had many an expedition together, not only to nascent houses, but also to lumber yards, vacant lots, the City Stables, and the Paving Department—the City

Stables, full of rather awful elephantine creatures, sedately stamping their huge feet; the Paving Department, with its Rocky Mountain ranges of cobblestones. As to the vacant fields, they were not really vacant; for carelessly recumbent, like sleeping giants, lay dozens of pile-drivers, ready to be commandeered as ships to sail to the Indies and the Gold Coast. Most fertile in possibilities, perhaps, and surely most fragrant, were the countless high heaps of boards in the yards along the water side of Atlantic Avenue; no other contrivance of man or nature lends itself quite so readily to climbing—not up the even sides, of course, but over the irregular ends, where adventure is linked with safety. One winter, from the top of these eminences, I could see the Harbor all frozen so hard that carriages and carts could drive across.

While I played, my father would sit and read—willing, however, when called upon, to interrupt his perusal and join me in my world of fantasy. He always carried in his pocket some small book to which he could revert in moments of leisure. Sometimes it was Todhunter's *Conic Sections*, sometimes the *Colloquia* of Erasmus (I still have those three little Erasmus volumes). As a determining factor, the subject was of less importance than the size, for pockets are limited and his interest was not. Like a medieval scholar, he longed to embrace *omne scibile*—and to make no use of it. Latin he read as naturally as any of the several modern languages he had mastered; and he was quite at home in Arabic. For historical data he could always give you chapter and verse, mostly from books (he had his Suetonius by heart), but occasionally from his own experience. One day, when I was studying American history of the time of the Mexican War, and asked him some question about the battle of Monterey, he answered with unexpected detail, and added quietly: "I was in that battle." Never before had I suspected that he had ever been a soldier, although I did know that he had been a lawyer and surveyor. His real specialty, however, was mathematics; but there was no consistency in his tastes. An avowed disciple of Voltaire, he loved the German Romanticists and used to delight my childhood by translating to me from Tieck, Hoffman, and Hauff. He knew all the Bible stories, too, and told them to me while I looked at the pictures. And often of a Sunday he would accompany my mother and me (not bereft, I am sorry to say, of the inevitable little volume) to the old chapel in Indiana Place.

THE NEW WORD

THIS was the title of a play—a world-war play—by Barrie. As you may remember, it deals with that peculiar form of bashfulness which, among "Anglo-Saxons," impedes any show of affection between father and son. The phenomenon is real enough. Such shyness, indeed, pervades more or less all amicable relations between English-speaking males; it manifests itself with greatest constancy and acuteness in the reciprocities of paternal-filial intercourse. This curious inhibition furnishes an amusing by-plot to Barrie's *Little Mary*—as far as I know, its first appearance on the stage. But in the diminutive war-time piece above mentioned, it is the whole thing. Hardly would the sentiment have been possible without the bellicose background. A young man, you recall, is going to the front, whilst his sire is compelled to stay at home. Through all the hasty preparations and all the leave-taking, the two go fumbling in stupid masculine fashion, anxious to avoid expression of a feeling which to both seems a weakness, but which in the end proves itself too strong. The "new word," of course, is "love."

A father to his flock was the late Charles W. Eliot, President of Harvard University. Big abstract ques-

tions of policy and big concrete problems of manage-
ment were always with him; but they could never
quench his curiosity about his individual fellow-
beings nor his interest in their welfare. As he grew
older, that interest assumed more and more a fatherly
tone; and, being fatherly, was subject to fatherly
reticence. Once, when I was still a youthful member
of his corps, he asked me suddenly: "Do you know
Dr. So-and-So?" So-and-So was younger yet. "Yes,"
I promptly replied. "Do you know him well enough
to offer advice?" With less briskness, but still confidently, I answered "Yes." "Then," he went on,
"I wish you would advise him on a matter of immediate and vital importance. I am told that he is
heating his study with a gas stove. Now gas stoves
poison the air"—and he explained to me scientif-
ically just how they did it. "These fumes undermine
the health and may cause death. He ought to be
persuaded to stop it." That mission I undertook,
storing in my memory some of the technical terms
which I instinctively felt to be effective, little as I
understood them, my study of chemistry having been
limited to the compass of three days immediately
preceding my examination in that subject. At any
rate, my demonstration was sufficiently learned to
accomplish its purpose. So-and-So is still alive, a
famous scholar half-way along in his fifties. And to
this moment he does not know who saved his life.

With the academic celebration of President Eliot's

ninetieth birthday came enthusiastic tributes of
praise and devotion from many parts and many
people. He listened, presumably with merited satisfaction, certainly not without amazement. What most
surprised him, he declared in his response, was the
word "love," which again and again recurred in the
eulogies bestowed upon him. Long and steadfastly
he had striven to do his duty in an important post,
and he was glad to have won respect, but he had
never thought of himself as capable of inspiring love
in his fellow-workers. It was a new word and evidently a touching thought.

Among other testimonials of esteem, on that occasion, was a fund for the purchase of books of his
choosing, for the University Library, the volumes to
be grouped under his name and to be marked with a
distinctive bookplate. That bookplate it was which
made the trouble. We wanted it to bear his likeness.
Photograph after photograph was submitted to him
for an indication of his preference; more than one
design was tried; more than one artist labored. He
disapproved of all. At last it was decided that a single
person should interview him and endeavor to learn
what sort of thing he might willingly accept. I was
that delegate, being at the time President of the
Harvard Alumni Association. "It is futile," he explained, "to attempt to hand anyone down to pos-
terity by a portrait, or, indeed, to perpetuate any
man's memory by a monument of any kind. We do

our work and pass on; others succeed us. A monument, if it is in itself a useful thing, may stand for a
while, but it quickly loses all connection with the
individual man for whom it was intended. Time gets
us all. No one should expect to be remembered.
Time gets us all." "Time may get us all eventually,"
I admitted, "but some it will get everlastingly late."
He smiled. "You say so," he replied, "because you—
because—" he stammered, I can almost swear he
blushed—"because"—the new word would not
come—"because you have known me so long."

In all those long years I never knew him to mistake the date of an appointment—except once, and
that was very near the end. Even then, as was to have
been expected, he came too early and not too late.
This is how it happened. He had promised to give a
public talk in some room in Emerson Hall on a certain afternoon at four-thirty. Somehow, the hour was
entered in his memoranda as "four." At four, then,
he was on the spot, a bit taken aback to find no
official there to welcome and present him. Audience
there was, a-plenty; people had crowded in early,
to get seats, and by four o'clock the room was
crammed. Quite unsuspecting, he entered, took a
chair on the platform, and, after waiting a few minutes for an announcer, proceded to introduce himself. His discourse met with eager approval, as his
speeches generally did, and he sat down amidst
protracted applause. Several dignitaries, to be sure,

had come in while his talk was in mid-course, and, perceiving what was afoot, had quietly seated themselves. No misgivings, therefore, assailed him until all was over, when a reporter drew near and thus delivered himself: "Do you know, Dr. Eliot, that you began half an hour before the time? We Representatives of the Press were awfully disappointed to lose the beginning, which, I am sure, was just as good as the close. See, nearly all the people are still here. Would you mind giving the first half over again?"

Such incidents as this, Dr. Eliot used to confide to Miss Grace Norton, his cousin and coeval, whom he visited from time to time. It was from her that I heard the foregoing story; also—freshly after the event—the following. Passing through Harvard Square, he encountered a group of little boys, and, short-sighted though he was, observed that one of them, the smallest, was crying bitterly, while the others were laughing. "What is the trouble?" he inquired sympathetically, stooping into proximity to the sufferer. "They all make fun of me because I have a scar on my face," was the whimpering reply. "Cheer up!" said the Doctor. "It is hard at first, I know; but after a while you will get used to it and scarcely mind it at all. Why, look at me," he added, pointing to his purple cheek; "I have had this great ugly mark all my life."

In his own grandchildren and great-grandchildren he took undisguised delight—or, to use his favorite word, "satisfaction." With the third generation, our "Anglo-Saxon" law of emotional prohibition ceases to be effective. That is why the grandfather's lot is so much happier than the father's. "What is Professor Knowitall doing nowadays?" he used to ask me, whenever we met in those latter years. He was not especially fond of Professor Knowitall, who was sometimes petulant in Faculty meetings; but he rightly esteemed that great scholar as a prodigy of learning and an ornament to the University, and habitually pictured him as an inveterate though rather succulent book-worm. "What is Professor Knowitall doing nowadays?" After the first time, I divined the answer he wanted to hear, and consequently always shaped my response as follows: "They tell me," I would reply, "that he spends a good part of his days playing with his grandchildren." Invariably a peal of merriment would follow, long and side-shaking. I do verily believe that something of Dr. Eliot's achievement of great age was due to his vivifying enjoyment of the image of Professor Knowitall playing with his grandchildren. One touch of grandfatherliness made them kin.

In another respect President Eliot resembled the Professor: he seldom made a mistake. Of his punctuality I have already spoken; almost equally unerring was his judgment of character. The more interesting, then, is a semblance of exception. This narrative having set forth one chronological aberration (on the

right side, to be sure), proper balance seems to require an instance of apparent psychological mis-
reading. No, I am not now referring to his consistent
kindness to myself; my rôle in the present chronicle
is merely that of a near-Boswell. I may, though, refer
(since the occasion spontaneously offers itself) to
his very flattering opinion that I was the preordained
candidate for a certain reputable office then vacant.
I may say in passing that nothing would have induced me to take the job. This is not sour grapes; the
post in question would have compelled me to be on
my good behavior all the time, a poor exchange for
the more moderate requirements of my actual position. This, however, I tactfully refrained from saying.
But the answer I did make was even more tactless
than that would have been. "No," I protested, "I am
too old." "Too old!" he cried in derision. "Why, I
doubt whether you are sixty yet!" With the pride of a
youth who has just attained majority, I hastened to
assure him that I really was sixty, having reached
that enviable age the week before. "Then," he declared, "you undoubtedly are the man."

No, that is not the tale I meant to tell. The intended story is serious, almost tragic. It was long,
long, ago, in the days when he was President and I
was chairman of a Department. In response to an
urgent request, I was seated in his private office. "I
am sorry," he began, "to have to make a most un-
pleasant communication. The matter, though very

delicate, is too important to be overlooked. Report
has reached me from a reliable quarter that one
member of your staff is causing some talk by conspicuous attention to ladies other than his wife. Now,
this ought to be stopped. Will you stop it?" As an
indispensable preliminary, I inquired who the offending party was. Nobody—unless I should divulge
a secret which I have sworn to keep—nobody can
conceive of my wonderment when I heard the name.
Suffice it to say that the bearer was the very last
person of whom such things could be true. The President had really no personal acquaintance with him,
but I knew him very well—so well that my one im-
pulse, almost uncontrollable, was a desire to laugh.
With an approximately straight face, however, I
assured him that there must be a misunderstanding.
What that misconception was, I subsequently labored
Holmes-like to discover; and I contrived a theory—a
theory involving two verbal twists in transmission—
which I still believe may cover the case; but I cannot
expound it further without betrayal. Dr. Eliot, un-
shaken by my expostulation, begged me to make sure
that the alleged misconduct should come to an end.
I promised. At our next Department meeting, then,
when the regular business was done, I announced
that one among us had been denounced to the President for paying undue attention to extraneous married ladies. It must stop, I added. Of course, I mentioned no name. Amazement seized me once more.

The result of my speech was the opposite of my expectation: instead of controlled but general merriment, an atmosphere of general consternation encompassed us. Speechless gloom, unbroken by word or smile. Tityrus turned ghastly pale, and I apprehended a violent fit of nausea. Corydon nervously plucked the stuffing out of his armchair. Strephon, who had just begun helping himself to a glass of beer, poured the fluid on the window-sill and the wallpaper. Thyrsis crumpled up on the sofa. Daphnis, a bachelor, sat wide-eyed and open-mouthed. Cacus (surnamed Fumifer) let his cigar go out. And Amyntas, remaining behind on some pretext after the others had departed, with a heart-breaking affectation of jocoseness inquired whether he was the one. He was not. Never, even after my death, shall the identity of the pseudo-Lothario be revealed. At any rate, the evil report fortunately was not repeated. Decades later, breaking a long-sealed silence, I related the incident at a dinner where nearly all the parties implicated—and thirty or so uninvolved—were present. Before me sat the quondam defendant, innocently unconcerned, vaguely wondering who (if anyone) the supposed culprit might be. But he shall never know.

Far from typical in its implication of a mistake or a mystery, this happening was characteristic of Dr. Eliot's unremitting watchfulness for public good and private weal. The very last summer he was able to be about, he called at my cottage in the course of an extraordinary and highly dubious expedition on behalf of his family and neighbors. Across the water, about three and a third miles (in a bee line) from his vacation home, is a picturesque projection called Seawall Point; and thereupon had recently been constructed a house, which by reason of its situation and its whiteness was startlingly conspicuous, quite altering the contour line in that direction. Eyes long accustomed to loving communion with the view from President Eliot's verandah could not be reconciled to the intrusion. Dissatisfaction, indeed, became so intense that he, who never could perceive an evil without devising a remedy, parted on an errand which to the vulgar would seem Quixotic. It must be remembered that his sight, always restricted in range, was by that time almost gone; his mission, then, was entirely altruistic. It was nothing less than an appeal to the owner of the offending structure to mitigate its self-assertiveness by painting it green. The upshot was a compromise: the proprietor, though reluctant to sacrifice a new coat of white, agreed to disguise its brightness with a screen of shrubs and vines.

Real Quixotism is a blend of the noble and the comic. Should anyone imagine that in this adventure the protagonist was unaware of the comic element, he would be mistaken. Earnest as he was, he had his good share of humor. The things that most amused him were inconsistencies in conduct and incongruities in vocabulary. Once, in the midst of a Faculty meeting, he was thrown into a violent fit of mirth while reading aloud an admonition, just received from a venerable and notoriously forgetful fellow-educator, to the effect that "we must look backward into the past and forward into the future." At another reunion of our body, the Department of Mathematics asked permission to change the title of one of its courses from "The functions of a complex variable defined by an ordinary differential equation of the first order and the first degree" to "Expansion in series of polynomials of a complex variable." After a lapse of thirty years, I cannot be sure that I have cited these rubrics aright; but they were something like that. In those long-vanished days, our Faculty was ready to debate anything and to raise objections to any proposition, of whatsoever nature, that might be brought before it by anybody. On this occasion, though, the President forestalled acrimonious dissension by observing: "Of the two, the new title appears somewhat the more seductive."

Interest in landscape—illustrated by his Seawall Point crusade—was strong in him, induced partly, I think, by love of his son Charles, the landscape architect. Interest in education was of course his main concern, and he made himself familiar with every phase of pedagogy, from the out-of-door school to the German university. "Do you hear anything about the

Shady Hill School?" he asked me once, already near his nineties. "My only direct testimony," I replied, "came to me one day last week from a little boy of five or six, a pretty child whom I had never seen before. He stopped me abruptly on the street, with the remark: 'I bet you don't know where I go to school.' 'No,' I admitted. 'What school is it?' 'The Shady Hill School; and it's the best school in the world.'" "No recommendation could be better than that," cried Dr. Eliot enthusiastically. He never forgot the episode. Every time I saw him thereafter he would ask: "Have you met your little Shady Hill friend again?" Invariably I had to answer "No." The dear child had disappeared from my life as suddenly as he had come into it. Once, when Mr. Eliot had recurred to the theme, he said: "Do children often come to you, as he did, and speak to you unasked?" "Why, yes," I answered, reflectively, "I believe they do." Indeed now that I think of it, I seem to have been something of a magnet (not always a willing one) for children, stray dogs, and drunken men. "They don't come to me," he wistfully went on. "I wonder why it is. Can you explain why they speak to you and not to me?" "Perhaps they feel themselves very far away from so tall as man as you," was the best I could improvise. And I doubt whether I could do better now. There was a certain tallness about him which, quite without his volition, made his associates conscious of their littleness. But there was in him no lack of all the "new word" signifies.